The
Connell Guide
to
Milton's

Paradise Lost

by
Caroline Moore

Contents

NOTES

Introduction

Dr Johnson sums up the case against Milton: "the want of human interest is always felt." It is the apparent distance of *Paradise Lost* from ordinary humanity that has thrilled or repelled critics throughout the ages. While many readers are carried away by Milton's sublimity, others are daunted by his grandeur, scope and learning.

Milton himself declared that he would not begin to write until he had "completed the full circle of my private studies". The Greek word for a circle of learning is the root of "encyclopaedia"; and Milton's erudition is encyclopaedic. *Paradise Lost* draws on both ancient learning and the scholarship of his day, displaying not only his deep knowledge of the Bible and Biblical scholarship, and his passionate assimilation of the classics, but also his absorption in astronomy, cosmology, geography, numerology and science.

Yet many critics of *Paradise Lost* argue that all this circling lacks a human centre. Who, after all, is the hero? Adam and Eve in their unfallen state are too remote from us; Christ is not yet incarnate; God cannot be a character. Which leaves us with the magnificently problematic figure of Satan.

This book will suggest that, contrary to what these critics argue, the core of *Paradise Lost* is extraordinarily human. Milton himself believed that poetry excelled at describing "the wily subtleties and refluxes of man's thought from within". This is precisely what *Paradise Lost* does. If, to a generation raised on the novel, Milton's methods of psychological exploration seem strange, this only intensifies the effect: *Paradise Lost* is a poem that explores the dark byways and infinite strangeness of the human heart.

The Garden of Eden - An Old Blind Man Sits Thinking, *by John Millar Watt (1895-1975). Illustration of Adam and Eve in the garden of Eden, based on John Milton's Paradise Lost. "About them frisking play'd All beasts of th' Earth."*

A summary of the plot

BOOK I

Begins with an invocation [*invocatio:* a prayer to the Muse], combined with a setting out of the scope of the poem ("the whole subject").

The first scene opens in hell, with Satan and his angels still dazed, "confounded", by their fall from heaven. Satan rouses himself and his troops, whose names are paraded; and the devils construct the place of Pandaemonium as their council hall.

BOOK II

The Council in Hell: the devils debate whether and how to wage war on God. Satan volunteers for the mission of finding and ruining God's latest creation, man. He journeys to the gates of hell, where he meets his self-begotten daughter, Sin, and his incestuously- conceived son/grandson, Death.

Sin opens the gate, and Satan plunges into the realm of Chaos and Old Night. At the end of the book, he glimpses the tiny "pendant world" of the newly-created universe.

BOOK III

The scene shifts to heaven. God points out Satan to his Son, and foretells his success in perverting mankind. The dialogue between God and his Son that follows is a *theodicy*: it explains the doctrines of free-will and grace, to affirm God's justice and mercy in allowing this to happen. Christ volunteers for the divine mission to ransom mankind; God ordains his incarnation; and angels celebrate Father and Son.

Meanwhile, Satan penetrates the outermost hollow orbs of the universe, arrives at the orb of the sun, and deceives the angel on watch there, Uriel, by disguising himself as a cherub to gain directions to earth.

BOOK IV

Satan alights on Mount Niphates and "falls into many doubts with himself." Confirmed in his evil, he trespasses into Paradise. "The garden described; Satan's first sight of Adam and Eve; his wonder at their happy form and state". Eve describes to Adam her first awakening.

Eavesdropping on their conversation, Satan learns of the existence of a forbidden tree, and hatches his plot. Satan's disfiguring passions allow Uriel to see through his disguise; and Uriel descends to warn Gabriel.

Adam and Eve, marvelling at the stars, go hand in hand to their "blissful bower", where they enjoy uninhibited and perfect sex, and fall asleep.

Gabriel on patrol discovers Satan in the form of a toad, squatting by the ear of sleeping Eve and infecting her dreams. Satan defies the angelic guard, but then flees.

BOOK V

Eve tells Adam of her dream-temptation; he comforts her. They hymn the morning, and begin work. God sends the archangel Raphael down to instruct and "admonish" Adam. He tells the story of Satan's original rebellion against God, and of the good angel Abdiel who stood firm against apostasy.

BOOK VI

Raphael continues his narrative, telling of the war in heaven. By the second day, the battle reached stalemate; on the third day, God sent his Son in a triumphal war-chariot, and the devils were driven into the abyss.

BOOK VII

Invocation to heavenly muse. Raphael recounts the creation of the world.

BOOK VIII

Adam questions Raphael about astronomy, but is "doubtfully answered." Eve leaves to tend her flowers, and Adam relates his memories of his own creation and first meeting with Eve. Raphael and Adam discuss human and angelic love and sex.

BOOK IX

Satan returns at midnight in the form of a mist, and enters into the sleeping serpent. In the morning, Eve proposes that she and Adam should work separately;

Adam disagrees, but yields. Satan finds Eve working alone, and tempts her. She eats the forbidden fruit; and Adam resolves "through vehemence of love to perish with her." He too eats, and the couple are overcome by quasi-drunken lust, and fall sleep. They awake to bitter mutual recriminations.

BOOK X

God sends his Son to judge the transgressors. Sin and Death break out of hell and build a bridge to earth. Satan enters hell in triumph, but is greeted only by a "general hiss", as he and all his devils are transformed into snakes.Sin and Death begin their ravages; God foretells the final victory over them. Adam and Eve move from despair to repentance, and the book ends with their prayers to God.

BOOK XI

Christ intercedes for Adam and Eve. God sends Michael to expel them from Paradise; but first he reveals and explains to Adam the future history of mankind.

BOOK XII

Michael continues his history lesson, up to the incarnation, crucifixion and resurrection of Christ, and the subsequent corruption of the Church before his Second Coming. Adam and Eve (who has been asleep, but was instructed in her dreams) are expelled from Paradise.

What is *Paradise Lost* about?

Paradise Lost is about the act of choice – and, above all, about the deeply peculiar psychology involved in the act of knowingly choosing wrong.

Milton placed the act of choice not just at the centre of his poem but at the heart of all morality. It was, for him, at the centre of what it is to be human, and what it means to be free. Man is god-like in his reason, and "Reason also is choice". [III. 108] When God gave Adam reason – Milton wrote in his pamphlet against censorship, *Areopagitica* – "he gave him freedom to choose, for reason is but choosing; he had been else a mere artificial Adam, such an Adam as he is in the motions". Without free will, in other words, Adam would be a mere puppet.

Milton's passionate belief in free will was unusual for the period, and deeply unorthodox for a radical Puritan. In Milton's day, indeed, the belief that fallen human beings were free to choose – and by their choices determine whether they were saved or damned – was controversial enough to attract its own theological label, Arminianism.

Most Civil War Puritans were, unlike Milton, broadly Calvinist in outlook. They believed that human choice, even human morality, is irrelevant, that salvation depends solely upon God's will, and that the elect are so secure in their election that it is impossible for them to sin. (It is one of the paradoxes of Calvinism that a creed which apparently undermines the need for human striving should nevertheless have spawned the Protestant work ethic.)

In fact, Calvin's doctrine threatens to deny the individual any role at all in salvation – and this Milton did not accept. Yet to modern ears, the alternative, Arminianism, sounds equally harsh. For Milton, life was one long series of tests – a rigorous divine exam system, in which, if a sinner failed, it was his fault alone. He might, through strenuous repentance, be allowed to sit a retake, but he could never know that he had passed until death. Most individuals, in Milton's stern view, would be likely to fail.

Coleridge summed up the paradoxes of Arminianism and Calvinism:

> Arminianism is cruel to individuals, for fear of damaging the race by false hopes and improper confidences, while Calvinism is horrible for the race, but full of consolation for the suffering individual...

One should never forget that when Milton wrote *Paradise Lost,* he was writing in the shadow of failure, fallen "on evil days... and evil tongues". [VII. 26] His political hopes had been overthrown; the Royalists had returned in triumph. He was blind, impoverished and, worst of all, facing the possibility that since the "Good Old Cause" he championed had been defeated, it had never been favoured by God.

Now he was himself in search of "consolation for the suffering individual", and hoping to find in the heart of his "cruel" Arminian creed something akin to the sweet comforts of Calvinist assurance. In his search he was forced to look deep into the mysteries that lie behind every individual act of choice.

Paradise Lost is full of seemingly arbitrary decisions: Satan's to rebel; Eve's to eat the apple; Adam's to follow her. Why does an omniscient God leave us free to choose, in order to prove our faith, if He already knows we will err and fall? If our choices are known before we make them, are they really choices at all? These, of course, are well worn theological conundrums, to which there are equally well known replies. What Milton imagines afresh in *Paradise Lost*, however, is the human psychology of the Fall. He is fascinated by how and why we can make catastrophic choices when we know, even as we make them, that they will probably lead to disaster.

These are the questions which interested Milton, and which he explored with such sensitivity and humanity in *Paradise Lost*. In the process, he redefined the epic – and redefined, too, the whole notion of heroism.

How does *Paradise Lost* fit into the tradition of epic poetry?

The *Iliad* and the *Aeneid,* acknowledged by Milton as his "diffuse models" for the epic form, are full of myths and improbable events. But epics, as even Aristotle somewhat grudgingly conceded, can encompass the "improbable", since they do not have to be physically enacted on the stage. They are also freed from the need for a straightforward narrative, enacted by real people moving about the stage in real time. Epics can become relatively atemporal, looping through time, veering into apparent digression, holding up the narrative to indulge in extended epic similes. Dramatic suspense may be undermined, but Homer's listeners would have already been familiar with the story of the fall of Troy.

And there were compensations for rewriting an ancient story, as Isabel MacCaffrey suggests:

> The poet whose subject is myth strives to promote... not learning but knowledge... to produce not development but revelation, not an introduction to something new, but a deepened understanding of something old. Consequently, the "normal" straightforward narrative patterns traditional to story tellers will be inappropriate; suspense will be

replaced by the tacit comment of interconnecting temporal threads.

Paradise Lost uses to the full the imaginative depth allowed by the epic form. As MacCaffrey suggests, the form frees Milton to imitate the atemporality of God himself, for whom "all times are eternally present".

What Milton is seeking is not suspense – but depth. *Paradise Lost* lives along each line, partly because each line is in living connection to the rest of the poem. Interconnecting threads of analogy criss-cross the filaments of narrative, and images which illuminate the murky processes of political decision-making during the Parliament of the Devils in Book I, for example, will resurface to cast light on the central act of choice in Book IX.

But even when *Paradise Lost* adheres most faithfully to the epic mould, there are crucial differences. Homeric and Virgilian epics tell of great deeds – of feats upon the battlefield and journeys of heroic endeavour, encompassing the loss and founding of nations. In *Paradise Lost*, on the other hand, the epic form spirals around a supremely unheroic action – picking an apple. Milton is attempting to redefine the epic to exalt a different, Christian form of courage – "the better fortitude/Of patience," [IX. 31-2] – which depends

Opposite: Blake's illustration of The Temptation and Fall of Eve, 1808

not upon action but restraint, and portrays the winning or losing not of a nation, but of the inward kingdom of the soul.

Milton does not follow the path by which other Christian writers attempted to reclaim the epic form. He does not, for example, use the kind of Christian allegory that is at the heart of epics like Spenser's *Faerie Queen,* or *The Purple Island,* written by Spenser's 17th-century follower Phineas Fletcher.

Both works caught Milton's imagination, as echoes in his poetry show. But Milton, as his contemporary Andrew Marvell recognized in his poem "On Mr Milton's 'Paradise Lost'", did something entirely and remarkably different. "Blind, yet bold", he did not try to show Genesis "in a play", nor did he "ruin... the sacred truth to fable and old song". He chose a form which was neither dramatic nor allegorical, boldly trusting in the "sacred truth" of his myth (see opposite).

Though never literal-minded in his interpretation of the Scriptures, Milton believed what was written in the Bible, and his belief in the essential, overarching truth of his story governs the form of *Paradise Lost.*

It also turns the function of epic similes and digressions inside out. In Homeric epic, the listener is taken on mind-stretching mythic journeys, across monster-filled oceans or on to battlefields where gods interact with heroes who are greater than ordinary mortals; and Homeric similes work by contrast. They are apt to be homely: pleasant little islands of everyday imagery where the hearer's mind can rest on its voyaging, anchored in the real world.

In *Paradise Lost* there is no rest for the weary. Milton's epic similes are themselves notoriously mind-stretching: they reach out to pagan fable, to exotic lands, to new worlds of astronomic discovery. Homeric similes look back to Greek homesteads, where corn is scythed and turtledoves peck in the sun, and the numerous dangers are home-grown and concrete (such as lions carrying off goats under the noses of the goatherd's dogs). They are given "a local habitation and a name"*. Miltonic similes rarely even glance at England, and their dangers are thrillingly murky.

LITERAL OR METAPHORICAL

Seventeenth-century Protestants believed the Bible was literally true; yet they were often less literal-minded than some modern evangelicals. They knew that "the letter killeth", and that God often spoke in parables and metaphors in order to drive them beyond literal-mindedness,

Milton, for example, did not believe that the world was made in six days. This is only the way in which creation is "so told as earthly notion can conceive". [VII. 179] Like Augustine, Milton believed that creation was a single, instantaneous act.◆

MILTON'S EPIC SIMILES

Typical of Milton's mind-stretching imagery in *Paradise Lost* is his first extended simile. Satan is floating "chained on the burning lake", and the simile begins by comparing his "bulk" to that of the mythical Titans and Giants who took part in the war against Jupiter. Briareus and Typhon were both storm-gods: Briareus was a Titan with 100 arms and 50 heads, who is sometimes described as a sea god and sometimes endowed with a long, split, scaly tail; Typhon, a Giant, is described by Hesiod as a dragon possessing 100 serpent's heads, but sometimes has tentacle arms, and in Milton's *Nativity Ode* is described as "ending in snaky twine"; so these comparisons foreshadow Satan's later serpentine metamorphoses.

Thus Satan talking to his nearest mate
With head uplift above the wave, and eyes
That sparkling blazed, his other parts besides
Prone on the flood, extended long and large
Lay floating many a rood, in bulk as huge
As whom the fables name of monstrous size,
Titanian, or Earth born, that warred on Jove,
Briareus or Typhon, whom the den

By ancient Tarsus held, or that sea-beast
Leviathan, which God of all his works
Created hugest that swim the ocean stream:
Him haply slumbering on the Norway foam
The pilot of some small night-foundered skiff,
Deeming some island, oft, as seamen tell,
With fixed anchor in his scaly rind
Moors by his side under the lea, while night
Invests the sea, and wished morn delays...
[I. 192-208]

Milton's opening comparison leaves the reader's imagination straining: it does not help us to visualize Satan's dimensions, since no one knows the actual size (or shape) of Briareus or Typhon. Nor does it help much when Milton moves from the fabulous though anatomically confusing snaky monsters of pagan myth to the 'real' monster, Leviathan – which is of course 'true' because it is mentioned in the Bible.

Commentators were divided over whether the monster or "sea-beast" was a sea-dragon or a whale: Milton does not help us to decide.
We only know that it is "slumbering on the Norway foam": a description that ridiculed by the 18th-century editor Richard Bentley ("it must be very solid Foam, that can support a sleeping Whale"), but defended by Christopher Ricks : "There is something sinister and mysterious, something of black magic, about Satan the Leviathan." And then there is that unnerving detail of the creature

having a "scaly rind". Rind is brilliantly strange: is it skin or bark? Is this unknown beast from the deep animal or vegetable?

This wavering uncertainty is exactly the sort of effect singled out by critics who complain that Milton's Grand Style is magnificent but imprecise. But that is a bit like complaining that a director of a monster movie does not let you see the monster clearly from the beginning: imprecision here is an effect that Milton is using – using, in fact, as a film director might, cutting between disturbing images: a general impression of something vague, writhing and vast out there in the dark; a clear shot of a tired human (doomed, of course); and then that jolting detail, a flash of something uncategorisably alien... And we never discover what happens to the pilot. The sense of danger in this simile is superbly managed. We are sharing the pilot's uncertainties, and if we too struggle, like a "small night-foundered skiff", Milton is evidently intending us to be, at the very least, disconcerted.
He is alerting us to the very real dangers of mistaking what is important, anchoring on the "scaly rind" without seeing the true nature of the beast – and of becoming fixated on the beguiling surface of pagan fable rather than seeing Christian truth.◆

Is Milton's handling of Satan flawed?

When Milton redefines the epic in *Paradise Lost,* he deliberately casts Satan at first as an unreconstructed epic hero. Satan has all the virtues of an Achilles: undaunted courage, charisma, and magnificent rhetoric. These are stirring yet morally undirected qualities – found equally in Nelson Mandela or Hitler. In his handling of Satan, Milton has been accused of losing control of his material and even, in Blake's famous phrase, being "of the devil's party without knowing it". But if Satan does display elements of true heroism – albeit limited and misdirected – this is because his Fall is not yet complete. In the opening book, he is still magnificent:

...He above the rest
In shape and gesture proudly eminent
Stood like a tower; his form had not yet lost
All her original brightness, nor appeared
Less than archangel ruined, and the excess
Of glory obscured...

[I. 589-594]

One of the narrative arcs of *Paradise Lost* will show the progressive degradation of Satan, from the cloudy grandeur of "archangel ruined" down to imprisonment in the base form that he himself chooses, "a monstrous serpent on his belly prone". [X. 514]

This clear trajectory, however, prompts some readers to complain that Milton, far from losing control, subjects his material – and particularly Satan – to ruthlessly willed orthodoxy. In Milton's depiction of Satan, say these critics, the arch-fiend is never a free agent. But then we are never shown him before his fall; he has already chosen, wrongly, and is already doomed by his choice. He is "the father of lies" from the opening lines of *Paradise Lost*.

All of the action of *Paradise Lost* therefore takes place in a prolonged stay of execution – the delay before God punishes Satan. In the meantime, Satan acts only through God's "permissive will", and when he rears his head up from the burning lake in Book I, it is only because God allows it:

....nor ever thence
Had risen or heaved his head, but that the will
And high permission of all-ruling heaven
Left him at large to his own dark designs...
[I. 210-3]

And this is permitted only in order "that with re-iterated crimes he might / Heap on himself damnation." [I. 215] This is a peculiar form of control – where the puppet-master lets the strings go slack in order to allow his puppets

Sistine Chapel Ceiling (1508-12): The Fall of Man, 1510, Michelangelo Buonarroti. Milton runs counter to convention in not representing temptation as intrinsically female, or Eve as a temptress.

to become self-entangled.

There is some truth in the argument that Satan is never a free agent in *Paradise Lost,* since the self-defining choices he makes throughout the poem are always described in language that suggests compulsion. But this is because in Milton's universe choosing wrong always compromises integrity and freedom.

One does not have to believe, as Milton did, that true liberty and self-knowledge can only be found in choosing obedience to God's will to see the human force of this. We all know that acts of choice involve a narrowing of possibilities, and that it is possible to become entrapped even – or especially – by a moment's almost arbitrary decision that is in retrospect obviously wrong. A one-night stand, a drink too many before getting behind the wheel of a car...

And though Satan is often sympathetic in the early books, where he is magnificently flawed and defiant, Milton's descriptions of a reduced and self-entrapped Satan in the later books may compel – not sympathy, exactly – but recognition in the reader. Satan's despair is both moving and repellent (as perhaps all pure despair is, since by definition it lies beyond sympathy: despair would not be despair if it could be shared); and the compulsion that shapes his false and fallen choices is rendered with claustrophobic clarity. This is Satan on his own willed – and profoundly unheroic – choice to squeeze forcibly into the body of a serpent:

O foul descent! That I who erst contended
With gods to sit the highest, am now constrained
Into a beast, and mixed with bestial slime,
This essence to incarnate and imbrute,

That to the highth of deity aspired...
[IX. 163-7]

"Constrained" means compressed, but also forced. "Incarnate" contains of course a glancing contrast with Christ's entrance into human form – when God's son, not some aspiring imposter, undertakes the demeaning limitations of incarnation out of his own free-will, acting from love rather than malice. But if Christ acts of his own free-will, who "constrains" Satan?

The obvious answer must be Satan himself: the father of lies is again arguing "necessity, the tyrant's plea" [IV. 393-4], and at the same time indulging in unattractive self-pity. Even more powerfully, Satan's disgust ("bestial slime") embodies profound and despairing self-loathing. Yet the notion that Satan is "constrained" runs through the poem, and whether the reader takes this constraint as being external (forced on him by circumstances), or internal (the product of his own wicked nature), the danger is that God will seem to blame. God governs all circumstances, and God created the Devil "a murderer from the beginning". [John 8.44] Milton, however, makes the 'constraint' neither purely external, nor purely internal, but the inexorable result of a series of false choices. His depiction of Satan's decreasing capacity for choice is indeed profoundly ambiguous: Satan throughout is both free and constrained. This, however, is an accurate description of all our (fallen) lives. And if Satan retrospectively discovers what he has chosen, rather than being consciously aware of the choices he makes when he makes them, that too is a condition we can recognise.

Why does Milton move away from drama to portray the moment of choice?

Samuel Johnson used the language of a drama critic when he wrote that "the plan of *Paradise Lost* has this inconvenience, that it comprises neither human action, nor human manners". ('Manners' is the 18th-century translation of Aristotle's 'ethos', character in action.) The peculiarity of Paradise, however, is that it is supremely undramatic. It is a state which depends not upon action, but upon inaction – upon *not* doing something.

To many readers, Milton's attempt to fill up the empty space this leaves in the lives of Adam and Eve is unconvincing. Sex and gardening, they feel, are not enough. And even if there is a wealth of symbolic meaning in the gardening episodes, one can still feel that a life spent propping up roses would soon become tedious.

But while Milton may not be concerned with

"human actions", he *is* concerned with human action – with a single deed, performed in supremely undramatic solitude ("pausing awhile, thus to herself she mused" [IX. 744]). And while he is not concerned with human characters exactly, he *is* concerned with the human mind. The imaginative core of *Paradise Lost* is the still centre at the heart of the storm. It is the moment that fires Shakespeare's imagination: the unreal "interim" "between the acting of a dreadful thing, and the first motion". [*Julius Caesar,* 2. i. 63-4]

Milton, unlike Shakespeare, does not explore this suspended moment between acting and not acting from *within* the minds of his characters. The very movement of his verse keeps it external to any inward drama: his sentence structures rarely give a sense of the mind in movement, moving hesitantly towards an unforeseen conclusion.

Shakespeare is the master of such speech rhythms, where even saying the verse out loud involves the actor in the faltering thoughts of the character. Here is Macbeth, caught in that supremely Shakespearean (and Miltonic) moment between the acting of a dreadful thing and the first motion:

If it 'twere done, when 'tis done, then 'twere well
It were done quickly: if th'assassination
Could trammel up the consequence, and catch
With his surcease, success; that but this blow

Might be the be-all and the end-all – here,
But here, upon this bank and shoal of time,
We'd jump the life to come.

[Macbeth, I. vii. 1-7]

The struggle of the voice across the line-breaks; the twitchy repeated double 'ifs' and treble 'buts'; the confusing echoes of the "'twere" – "'tis" – "'twere" – "it were" construction; the very difficulty of pronouncing "with his surcease, success"; the breathy but baffled urgency of "here/But here", all involve the reader moment by moment in the self-trammelled movement of Macbeth's mind, caught on this "bank and shoal of time" but staring into eternity and the abyss of action. It is a brilliantly realised evocation of tangled inhibition – a 'trammelled' or hobbled horse is tied to nothing but itself – and jerky impulse.

The 'inward' soliloquy is self-evidently a highly effective way of showing the human heart of any act of choice. It is not, however, Milton's chosen way. Here is one example of just how far Milton's poetry can seem disconcertingly 'external'. Satan is choosing which beast to enter as a disguise, and picks on the serpent:

Him after long debate, irresolute
Of thoughts revolved, his final sentence chose,
Fit vessel...

[IX. 87-89]

Margot Fonteyn and Rudolf Nureyev rehearse an intricate scene by French choreographer Roland Petit for the new ballet Paradise Lost, *1967*

There is no irresolution in the construction of this sentence . We know from the first word what Satan's choice will be: 'Him', the serpent. If this makes Satan's revolving thoughts seem irrelevant, this is rather horribly apt. Satan chooses the serpent as a useful tool; but he is himself a "vessel of wrath fitted for destruction" [Romans 9.22], and a tool in the hands of God.

When Milton does turn to dramatic soliloquy,

HERETICAL MILTON

Milton's doctrines on the relationship between Father and Son were heretical. He did not believe in the Trinity, and denied that the Son was "consubstantial and co-eternal" with the Father. In *De Doctrina Christiana*, he describes the Son as the first created being, whose (lesser) divinity was bestowed on him by the single supreme Deity.

This is a 17th-century version of Arianism; and a dangerous doctrine to hold. At least eight heretics who denied the Trinity were burnt between 1548 and 1612.

In *Paradise Lost*, this heresy is embedded in the apparent orthodoxy of "He all his father full expressed". In the next line, this is twisted to have two meanings. It could be that Christ receives from God *only* that limited part of Himself that He chooses to express fully.

This is important for the depiction of choice in *Paradise Lost*: if Christ is a created being, rather than God Himself, his decision to volunteer on behalf of mankind becomes comparable to human choice. ◆

he makes it plain that this is a fallen genre. It is a mark of loneliness; and as God himself says "it is not good for man to be alone". [Genesis 2.18] To be alone is to be cut off not just from man but from God, and therefore from one's true self. The Devil soliloquises, but Adam and Eve do so only in the last moments before they fall.

God, in *Paradise Lost*, never talks to himself. God has, of course, an undoubted advantage: he talks to Christ, the Word who "all his father full expressed". [VI. 670] The long discussions between God and His Son are, on one level, Milton's image of perfect self-consciousness and true self-knowledge. (His views on the relationship between Father and Son were, however, unorthodox. See opposite.)

How do Satan's soliloquies portray his loss of free choice?

When the Devil soliloquises, he is not so much dramatic as melodramatic. Milton's representation of Satan's internal thoughts do not, like Shakespeare's in *Macbeth*, show someone stumbling towards self-knowledge. But then Milton does not believe that mere introspection can ever arrive at truth. Instead, the Devil's soliloquies show a gradual falling-away into posturing staginess.

Satan has five soliloquies, which, as the critic Barbara Lewalksi points out, "associate him with the flawed protagonists of the Elizabethan stage"; and his dramatic models become increasingly ignoble. In his first soliloquy, on Mount Niphates [IV. 32-113] Satan at first resembles "Dr Faustus in his last hour, or Claudius striving unsuccessfully to pray", but descends by the end to villain-hero, a Richard III delighting in evil for its own sake. By his next soliloquy [IV. 358-92], Lewalski claims that he has become Richard III crossed with Marlowe's Jew of Malta, Barrabas, a combination of villain-hero and revenge hero; in the third soliloquy [IV. 505-35], he no longer has the grandeur of a hero at all. He is a leering, plotting voyeur, closer to Iago than Macbeth. And in Book IX, his soliloquies fall off the theatrical scale of tragedy altogether. When he chooses to "imbrute" himself [IX. 163-71], he "has moved outside and below both the classical and the Elizabethan paradigms for tragedy," ending, in Book X, in what Lewalski describes as "a grotesque black comedy of God's devising".

The first of these soliloquies is one of the most apparently "dramatic" speeches in *Paradise Lost*, displaying the "contending passions" which Johnson complained were missing in the unfallen characters of Adam and Eve.

But it is even more interesting for what it does *not* do. Its dramatic qualities are controlled, constrained from the outset by the narrator's before-and-after summing-up, which is, as Aristotle would say, telling not showing. The reader, therefore, once again knows even before Satan deliberates exactly what the outcome will be. Satan is on the brink of "his dire attempt", which

> *...nigh the birth*
> *Now rolling, boils in his tumultuous breast,*
> *And like a devilish engine back recoils*
> *Upon himself; horror and doubt distract*
> *His troubled thoughts, and from the bottom stir,*
> *The hell within him, for within him hell*
> *He brings, and round about him, nor from hell*
> *One step no more than from himself can fly*
> *By change of place: now conscience wakes despair*
> *That slumbered, wakes the bitter memory*
> *Of what he was, what is, and what must be,*
> *Worse; of worse deeds worse suffering must ensue.*
> *[IV. 15-26]*

The syntax is powerfully mimetic of entrapment. The antimetabole (mirror-patterning) of "hell within him... within him hell" echoes the self-reflexive nature of his torment; the triple repetitions "hell... hell... hell..."; "worse... worse... worse" resound inexorably.

But if this summing-up is unexpectedly

powerful, the soliloquy that follows has disappointed those critics who hope for Shakespearean self-revelation. It is not only deliberately melodramatic ("Ah wherefore!" "Me miserable!"), but, disconcertingly, puts into Satan's mouth a rigidly 'correct' version of the Fall: "Pride and worse ambition threw me down..." Satan even contradicts his own claim that the devils are "self-begot, self-raised". [V. 800] Now he parrots official theology instead: "He deserved no such return / From me, whom he created what I was..." [V. 40-57]

Obviously, we are supposed to believe that Satan's "conscience" has prompted his recognition of the truth, but the soliloquy does not involve us in the processes by which he performs this *volte face*. The most powerful lines in Satan's soliloquy express not the inward flux of choice, but the impossibility of movement. He "chose freely"; now free choice is lost.

Me miserable! Which way shall I fly
Infinite wrath, and infinite despair?
Which way I fly is hell; myself am hell;
And in the lowest deep a lower deep
Still threatening to devour me opens wide
To which the hell I suffer seems a heaven.

[IV. 73-8]

The lines of internal debate which immediately

follow come closest to charting inward conflict. "O then at last relent..."

The opening sounds promisingly ambiguous – a plea both to God and to himself to soften into repentance. This could then have led into the internal drama of salvation: the conflict of better and worse selves, which in Marlowe's *Dr Faustus* is represented by the old-fashioned device of a Good Angel and a Bad Angel whispering into Faustus's ear ("Faustus repent, yet God will pity thee... Thou art a spirit, God cannot pity thee"). But Satan already *is* the Bad Angel, and the voice of repentance is barely given room:

> *O then at last relent: is there no place*
> *Left for repentance, none for pardon left?*
> *[IV. 79-80]*

The rhetorical question supplies its own answer ("none for pardon left"). The conflict is already over.

Adam, after his fall, enters the same rhetorically self-limited moral territory. At the point where he has recognised his sin, but before he can move beyond it to repentance, he too falls into soliloquy; he too is "in a sea of passion tossed", which casts up only stilted self-pity ("O miserable of happy!"); he too enters into an 'internal' debate conducted only in the most external and already-concluded terms:

...Him [God] after all disputes
Forced I absolve: all my evasions vain,
And reasonings, though through mazes, lead me
still,
But to my own conviction.

[X. 828-31]

He is already convinced of his own sentence.

Like Satan's soliloquies, this is powerful but bleakly external poetry. What is missing is intimacy. This does not exclude a sort of sympathy. It is all that Milton asks even for himself. When he describes his own plight – "fallen on evil tongues and evil days", politically isolated, bereft and blind – he does not seek to draw us into his despair. There are none of the re-enacted feelings, the gasps and staginess of Donne or Hopkins; no dramatic ploys to make us feel along with him. But this is in its own way effective. We are made to know that we cannot and do not share his blindness: his self-description insists upon sheer and shut-off loneliness.

He is excluded from the natural world, and the social one:

Thus with the year
Seasons return, but not to me returns
Day, or the sweet approach of even or morn,
Or sight of vernal bloom, or summer's rose,
Or flocks, or herds, or human face divine;

But cloud instead, and ever-during dark
Surrounds me, from the cheerful ways of men
Cut off, and for the book of knowledge fair
Presented with a universal blank
Of nature's works to me expunged and razed
And wisdom at one entrance quite shut out.
[III. 40-50]

"Quite shut out"; full stop. What could be more external, yet more compellingly bleak, than that?

How does Milton portray the effects of false choice?

Fortunately for *Paradise Lost*, Milton regarded allegory in the same way he regarded soliloquies – as a fallen genre. This, however, makes it one way in which he represents the effects of false choices. His poetic universe is gloriously rich in fluid symbols and myth, which curdle into allegory only upon deliberately chosen occasions.

One example is Satan's encounter in Book II with his self-begotten daughter, Sin, who sprang from Satan's head (as Athena did from Jupiter's), and with his son/grandson, Death, who was conceived when Satan raped his own daughter.

On his journey to Earth, Satan meets Sin at the portal of Hell. She is a conventionally allegorical figure, who:

...seemed woman to the waist, and fair
But ended foul in many a scaly fold
Voluminous and vast, a serpent armed
With mortal sting: about her middle round
A cry of hell hounds never ceasing barked
With wide Cerberian mouths full loud, and rung
A hideous peal: yet, when they list, would creep,
If aught disturbed their noise, into her womb,
And kennel there, yet there still barked and howled,
Within unseen.

[II. 650-9]

This starts as a familiar portrayal of deceptive evil, and, at least for the first four lines, is easy to visualize and to understand as an allegory: a beautiful woman with a sting in her tail could obviously signify the tempting attractions of sin and its deadly consequences. But the allegorical picture becomes harder and harder to visualize. Milton merges the figure of snake-tailed Sin with that of Scylla, the nymph who (in Sandys's translation of Ovid) "beheld her hips with barking dogs imbrac'd". The clarity of the emblematic picture further dissolves when the figure begins to move, so that the "hell-hounds"

opposite: Adam and Eve in the Garden of Eden, *from the* Très Riches Heures *du Duc de Berry, a fifteenth-century French illuminated manuscript. Eve and the snake share not only the same long tresses, but the same face. Milton goes against tradition by not casting Eve as a temptress.. This familiar iconography (woman with a snake's tail) is relegated by Milton to the false 'seemings' on the borders of Hell.*

The cartoonist James Gillray's parody of Paradise Lost*; William Pitt (1759-1806) fights with the Chancellor, Edward Thurlow (1731-1806); Queen Charlotte (1744-1818), depicted as a serpent, intervenes in favour of Pitt. Gillray cannot draw Milton's formless Death, and has to fall back on the cartoonist's shorthand, a skeleton.*

periodically "creep... into her womb."

If Sin rapidly becomes almost ludicrously unimaginable, this is intentional: the sentence ends, pointedly, with the words "within *unseen*", and Milton seems to be suggesting the inadequacies of the allegorical word-picture by which she has been represented. Her "formidable shape" is only inadequate 'seeming'. The true nature of evil has to be unimaginable, since it is in Christian theology purely negative: it is a falling away from God, and an absence not only of Goodness, but also of Being.

In the description of her companion, Death, Milton goes further, deliberately creating a non-figure which cannot be made into a pictorial emblem at all. Death, as Coleridge pointed out, is usually represented by a skeleton, "the hardest and driest image that it is possible to discover". Milton's Death is de-personified into sheer, sinister flux:

The other shape
If shape it might be called that shape had none
Distinguishable in member, joint, or limb
Or substance might be called that shadow seemed,
For each seemed either; black it stood as night,
Fierce as ten Furies, terrible as hell,
And shook a dreadful dart; what seemed his head
The likeness of a kingly crown had on.
[II. 666-673]

In Book II, the meeting of Satan, Sin and Death

ALLEGORY AND CATHOLICISM

Milton associates allegory with the Catholic Church, which offered formalised but cumbersome 'typological' readings of the Bible. When Sin and Death solidify their highly allegorical bridge between earth and hell, their art is "pontifical" and Death wields a "mace petrific" – punning allusions to the Pope and his mace of office.◆

combines dubious allegory with the imitation of (equally dubious) classical epic. Satan fails to recognise Death, his incestuous son/grandson, and the two are elaborately preparing to strike each other, when Sin, equally elaborately, intervenes. This is exactly the sort of highly stylized moment in epic poetry that Milton's contemporaries tended to read allegorically. When, in the *Iliad,* Athena seizes Achilles by the hair to prevent him from attacking Agamemnon, every educated 17th-century reader would have known that it was an allegory of reason forestalling rash action.

Athena's choice is a good one, but Milton's version – with Sin protecting Satan and Death - is a deliberately empty, warped parody of it, just as the unholy Trinity of Satan, Sin and Death are a parody of the Father, Son and Holy Ghost. What Milton is representing in this scene is a moment of fallen choice, in which evil figures choose wrongly and in doing so slip out of control. He uses the epic convention of "synecdoche" – where one part of a person or scene represents the whole – to make the hands of the protagonists seem to take on a life of their own:

...Each at the head
Levelled his deadly aim; their fatal hands
No second stroke intend...

[II. 711-3]

The "snaky sorceress", Sin, rushes between, crying out "'O Father, what intends thy hand...'" and warns that if father and son destroy each other they will accidentally fulfil the will of "him who sits above and laughs the while":

She spake, and at her words the hellish pest
Forbore, then these to her Satan returned:
So strange thy outcry, and thy words so strange
Thou interposes, that my sudden hand
Prevented spares to tell thee yet by deeds
What it intends...

[II. 735-40]

Satan's hand is prevented, and "yet" – or still – spares Death; but that "yet" is syntactically precarious. It simultaneously suggests that his hand may "yet", in the future, go on to tell "what it intends": by the end of this cumbersome sentence, Satan's hand threatens to break free of grammatical control. (And, of course, in the very long term, the consequences will break free of Satan's control too, and his actions *will* bring about the destruction of Death, just as Sin warned.) This use of synecdoche is a small effect, but one that echoes through the poem, in repeated references to hands that seem to act of their own volition. Eve possesses another "unsparing hand". [V. 344] At first, this is used only to suggest that she is a generous hostess, heaping up fruits for her angelic guest; but it foreshadows the moment to come when, in terrible slow motion, her hand reaches out to the forbidden fruit:

> *...her rash hand in evil hour*
> *Forth reaching to the fruit.....*
>
> *[IX. 780-1]*

One of the psychological states Milton explores in *Paradise Lost* is how we can come to feel so dangerously external to a moment of choice.

Why is the 'psychology of delay' so important in *Paradise Lost*?

Paradise Lost is structured around delay. There is the long wait until the plucking of the apple, which we are told in the opening lines is to come. After the Fall, there is the delay before punishment, waiting for expulsion from Paradise; while all of Satan's acts take place in the moral no-man's land between sin and final retribution. And the whole poem is written by Milton in a state of waiting, with the "better fortitude/Of patience", in hope of the only true Restoration, which after the failure of all his earthly political hopes, can only be the Second Coming of Christ.

Again and again, Milton evokes the slowing of time in moments of overloaded crisis. He is particularly fascinated by crises of delay.

Here is a typically Miltonic passage, one apparently irrelevant to the narrative – so much so that the narrator actually tells us it is beside the point. The fable of the fall of Mulciber (or Vulcan) is described, in imitation of Homer's description of the fall of Hephaistos. [*Iliad*. i. 591-5) He is

> *...thrown by angry Jove*
> *Sheer o'er the crystal battlements; from morn*
> *To noon he fell, from noon to dewy eve,*
> *A summer's day; and with the setting sun*
> *Dropped from the zenith like a falling star*
> *On Lemnos the Aegean isle: thus they relate*
> *Erring...*
>
> *[I. 741-7]*

The Fall of Mulciber is a magnificent slow-motion effect, peculiarly lacking in urgency. Time gels into space; and because noon is higher in the sky than morn, Mulciber even seems midway to float up, with the weightlessness of freefall. Dew is the softest and sweetest of falls, and a summer's day is both long, and carefree. All beautiful; all, apparently, utterly inappropriate for the terror of falling – except that anyone who has ever fallen from a height or crashed a car will know of that inner slowing of time, that strange detachment and lack of alarm, in that stretched moment of delay. The imaginative core of *Paradise Lost* is a crisis of delay – a suspended moment between acting and not-acting – explored through a series of parallel incidents, images and extended similes. Milton's epic similes, slowing the action, play a role in this exploration: it is no accident that they cluster most thickly in Books I and II and Book IX, which are most directly concerned with the psychology of choice.

Again and again, Milton uses this slowing effect simultaneously to intensify and stretch moments of doubt, suspense and hesitation before action. It is a form of psychological distortion (see opposite). When Satan is confronting Death, for example, the combatants are elaborately compared to

> *....as when two black clouds*
> *With heaven's artillery fraught, come rattling on*
> *Over the Caspian, then stand front to front*
> *Hovering a space...*
>
> *[II. 714-7]*

The whole simile of delay itself delays the action. The length of the sentence, only partly quoted above, strains the comparison until it too becomes mimetically "fraught". The formulaic introduction – "as when" – becomes charged with fresh precision: Milton is pinpointing an overloaded moment in time. The "space" is both spatial and

KEITH DOUGLAS'S 'HOW TO KILL'

A similar psychological effect to the one created by Milton is described by Keith Douglas in his poem 'How to Kill', which describes how easy it is to become detached enough to pull the trigger of a rifle in a war. It starts with a parable of how time slows when waiting to catch an arching lob ('parabola', an arc, is the root of 'parable'):

Under the parabola of a ball,
a child turning into a man,
I looked into the air too long.
The ball fell in my hand, it sang
in the closed fist: Open Open
Behold a gift designed to kill.

Now in my dial of glass appears
the soldier who is going to die.
He smiles, and moves about in ways
his mother knows, habits of his.
The wires touch his face: I cry
Now. Death, like a familiar, hears

and look, has made a man of dust
of a man of flesh. This sorcery
I do. Being damned, I am amused
to see the centre of love diffused
and the waves of love travel into vacancy.
How easy it is to make a ghost.

The soldier is able to become fascinated by the man he is about to kill, in slow-motion close-up, down the sight of his rifle - "now in my dial of glass appears / The soldier who is going to die" - and it is simple to fire when the cross-wires in the sights line up on the target. "The wires touch his face", which, hideously, is both intimately close and impersonal. It is a poem about "how easy it is to make a ghost", and how easy it is to slip from the moral centre of one's own being. "Being damned, I am amused".◆

temporal, both the distance between the clouds and the empty moment before they "join their dark encounter". [II. 718] But it also suggests the psychological space of unnatural detachment.

It is this "space" of doubt that Satan feels on the edge of decision: "That space the Evil one abstracted stood / From his own evil" [IX. 463-4]; it is the gap on "the rough edge of battle" in Book VI (in a fight between the armies of good and evil, described by Raphael):

> *For now*
> *'Twixt host and host but narrow space was left,*
> *A dreadful interval, and front to front*
> *Presented stood in terrible array*
> *Of hideous length...*
>
> *[VI. 103-7]*

In such hideously long moments, it is easy to slip into inappropriate detachment: the good angels in this crisis in Book VI are ambushed by evil because, Raphael says, "we suspense [i.e. undecided] / Collected stood within our thoughts amused." [VI. 580-1]

In *Paradise Lost*, this dangerous detachment in moments of choice is explored through recurrent images of distance, height, and, above all, of hovering. Hovering, hanging and floating are embodied in our very language as metaphors for indecision: things are "up in the air"; we are "in suspense". In *Paradise Lost*, recurrent images of hovering and floating in the air are used to explore how a decision can become detached from the moral realities in which it should be grounded.

The obvious focus of all the hoverings, soarings and irresolute hangings in *Paradise Lost* is Eve's dream flight in Book V. The dream has been sent by Satan, the first inward "motion" of evil within her innocent mind; and awareness of the danger she is in is heightened by the way the incident draws together threads of imagery running through the poem.

What makes Eve visit the forbidden tree?

In hell, floating and hovering are associated with devilish flux. The devils float "weltring" [I. 787] on the burning lake – tossing and writhing and blown by winds. Hell is a place of hideous uncertainties, where even physical categories are confounded: "fiery waves", "darkness visible", and land whose essence and solidity are questionable, " ... as if it were land that ever burned/With solid, as the lake with liquid fire". [I. 229]

Yet if Hell is portrayed as a state of irresolution, Paradise is not a place of fixities. It is experienced almost as a state of rich indecision. Milton's Eden is one of infinite potential, embodied linguistically in the multiple possibilities of his "fluid syntax". But, as Christopher Ricks has pointed out , shadows of the fall are there in the description of the perfections. Even the streams flow "with mazy error under pendant shades". [IV. 239] "Error" means merely "wandering", but the possibility of sin is hinted at too – and the overhanging "pendant" branches suggest impending darkness. The "mazy error" recalls the devils in Book XI, "in wandering mazes lost", whilst debating the philosophical intricacies of the problem of free will.

These shadows do not, in themselves, compromise the perfection of Paradise. Milton knows that strange and wayward thoughts may slide into any human mind, and potentialities need not compromise innocence:

Evil into the mind of god or man
May come and go, so unapproved, and leave
Nor spot or blame behind...

[VI. 1117-9]

This would be Milton's answer to the existential conundrum posed by André Gide in *Les Caves du Vatican.* Most of us have at least wondered what it would be like to commit murder; most of us, obviously, do not act upon mere random imaginings. Gide's anti-hero, Lafcadio, does: on sheer impulse, he pushes a stranger from a moving train. This *"acte gratuit"* is, another character argues, the only form of pure freedom, since it is not governed or ruled by conventional morals or even comprehensible motive. *"Songez donc: un crime que ni le passion, ni le besoin ne motive"* ['Think of it: a crime not motivated by either passion or need'].

Taking the apple in Paradise is the primal *acte gratuit.* Eve's dream-temptation represents the first, "unapproved" motion within her – a purely random imagining, since her reason is asleep, and she is ruled by "fancy". Satan, in the form of a toad, has been whispering into her ear; and the dream he sends prefigures the temptation in Book IX.

In her sleep, Eve is first lured by the sound of a "gentle voice", speaking like a flattering lover – a debased, Cavalier version of Adam's tenderness. She follows the voice, and with dream-like inconsequentiality finds herself "on a sudden" at the forbidden tree, now seeming "much fairer to my fancy than by day", with a figure "shaped and winged" like an angel at its foot. (This is the disguise in which Satan slipped past the supposedly alert angel Uriel; so Eve cannot be blamed for trusting him in her sleep.) The fake angel "with venturous arm" – synecdoche again – plucks the fruit; and Eve's instinctive reaction is "horror". In her deepest self, she neither wants nor needs to rebel. Satan's way of tempting her beyond this sticking point is psychologically subtle.

Why does Satan use height to tempt Eve?

How do you tempt a woman who is instinctively good and has all she could desire, and has "*ni le passion, ni le besoin*" – no passions or needs that might overpower her will? Satan can offer Eve nothing on this earth she does not have, except an apple – and Milton is careful to make the actual fruit neutral and negligible in its properties: it is Satan who imputes to it magical, mind-expanding powers.

Satan's temptation is a subtle one. He offers a world of vague but infinite potential, which is only an extension of what she already has: "happy though thou art / Happier thou mayst be" [V. 75-6]; and, of course, the promise that she may be able to escape the confines of this earth altogether:

....be henceforth among the gods
Thy self a goddess, not to earth confined,
But sometimes in the air, as we, sometimes
Ascend to heaven, by merit thine, and see
What life the gods live there, and such live thou.
[V. 77-81]

Who has not dreamt of flying? It is a dream of pure, existential freedom. Yet even here Milton is careful to make sure that Eve is tempted by nothing Paradise cannot supply – including, eventually, escape from an earthbound existence. In Book V, Raphael promises Adam and Eve that if they make the right choices, which include eating the right food – "no inconvenient diet nor too light fare" – their

> *bodies may at last turn all to spirit,*
> *Improved by tract of time, and winged ascend*
> *Ethereal as we; or may at choice*
> *Here or in heavenly paradises dwell.*
> *[V. 495-500].*

What Satan offers the woman who has everything is the dizzying prospect of having everything all together, without delay, "on a sudden", and "forthwith". Raphael offers only slow, and slowly earned, transmutation: a "tract" of time had in Milton's day very strong connotations of time protracted, dragged out (from the Latin, *trahir*). Only by careful stages, "in contemplation of created things,/By steps we may ascend to God." [V. 511-2] This is not Satan's way. He takes shortcuts: even when entering Paradise, he scorns "due entrance" and "at one slight bound high over leaped all bound". [IV. 180-1]

Eve's first dream-temptation could easily have been represented as a simple moral test. Impatience, have-it-all greed, and of course that moral catch-all, pride, threaten the virtues of prudence, temperance and faith. These faults are possible in Eve – potentially, at least – but the actual temptation is an obscurer urge.

When Satan in the dream almost force-feeds Eve the fruit, the danger she faces is symbolized by height:

> *...Forthwith up to the clouds*
> *With him I flew, and underneath beheld*
> *The earth outstretched immense, a prospect wide*
> *And various: wondering at my flight and change*
> *To this high exaltation.*
>
> *[V. 86-90]*

Eve, as Isabel MacCaffrey points out, "has been allowed for a moment to 'view all things at one view', like God". The potential dangers are clear in the poetry: the instability of "various" and "change", the suspect elation of "exaltation", with its connotations of exalted rank and false pride. The nearest earthbound man normally comes to this state is in the act of contemplation that precedes a choice, when multiple possibilities hang in the balance, and everything is still possible.

In our human world, the need to act – to do something, anything – is at its most mindless under the pressure of emptiness. Every teenager knows what it is to feel 'out of one's mind' with boredom.

Milton's Paradise, however, is not one of blank inactivity. The pressures, indeed, are not those of emptiness, but of overload. Eve's everyday life in Paradise is presented as a never-ending series of richly suggestive moral choices: whether choosing which fruits to serve an angelic guest, or pruning back "wanton" growth, she has to display constant discrimination. Every action she takes is laden with moral significance; every plant and bird and beast offers its lesson, from the drooping roses which need propping up with myrtle [V. 430-1] (signifying the dependence of mortal happiness upon conjugal virtue), to the stork and "prudent crane", "with mutual wing / Easing their flight" [VII. 429-30] (emblems of vigilance and mutual support).

Milton's Arminian idea of heaven offers realms of infinite choice – and this undoubtedly – and entirely deliberately – comes very close to the infinite flux or "welter" of indecision found in hell. However, hell offers, as always, a subtle perversion of what is truly good. Decisions in hell are non-choices, both endless and limited (simultaneously lost in and confined to labyrinths).

Yet the infinite choices offered in heaven are a daunting prospect. Humanity cannot bear infinite choice, and it is perhaps not surprising Eve falls from heaven's giddy heights.

Precisely because there is so much to take in, it is no wonder that at times Eve lets her attention slide, and even among her drooping roses can, fatally, be "mindless the while". Satan offers her release from the continual, Arminian pressures of choice in her reading of the world.

If an act to end all effort, a choice to end all choices, sounds suicidal, this is of course precisely what it is: Satan is urging Eve towards death. The image of great and unstable height seems particularly apt: the urge to throw oneself off a tall building is the strangest and darkest of compulsions. Edgar Allan Poe, famous for his interest in morbid psychology, cited it as the work of the "imp of the perverse" , and vertigo is, in 17th-century sermons, a metaphor for sinfulness and folly, "causing us to fall and stagger". Milton's Paradise of Fools includes Empedocles, who "to be deemed / A god, leaped fondly into Aetna flames", and Cleombrotus, "who to enjoy / Plato's Elysium, leaped into the sea". [III. 469-73]

In *Paradise Regained,* Milton uses height to explore the human urge simply to act. As the last temptation in the wilderness – and Milton had a choice of Gospel versions, so actively *chose* to make this his climax – Christ is placed by Satan on the vertiginous "highest peak" of the temple, and urged by Satan to cast himself down. "To stand upright will ask thee skill". [*Paradise Regained.* IV. 551] Not to act is shown as the hardest task of all. When Christ returns home, in a state of purely inward triumph, he is still "private, inactive, calm, contemplative"[*Paradise Regained* II. 81] – the most difficult state of all to maintain. He achieves "high attest" [*Paraidse Regained* I. 37] – the best possible proof or "attest" of his divinity is given by passing the test of height.

Maintaining this state of pure contemplation may be, as Thomas Aquinas said, "non proprie humana sed superhumana" – not suitable for men, but gods. For Milton, *not* acting, exercising self-restraint, was a choice too, but he knew how deeply it runs counter to our human need to prove ourselves in action. If the strains of waiting are a constant, almost obsessive theme in Milton's poetry and prose this is partly because they ran deep in his own life (see p.58).

Standing and waiting under these pressures is hard. There is a deep human need to do something, anything – even if it is as mindless as dropping a stone down a deep well or plucking an apple that hangs in tempting stillness. If this is a dark and counter-logical impulse, however, poetry is fitted to explore it. As Milton wrote, poetry is "subsequent, or indeed rather precedent" to logic.

A LATE STARTER

Milton was a late starter ("beginning late", IX. 26). He knew the burden of parental expectations; he had from his earliest years thought of himself, like Samson, "as of a person separate to God / Designed for great exploits". [*Samson Agonistes*. 31-2] He intended to be an immortal poet, and said so – he would outdo "the greatest and choicest wits of Athens, Rome, or modern Italy, and those Hebrews of old" in the poetic service of his country and the Christian faith. His "intentions" for a great work, he tells us, "have lived within me ever since I could conceive myself anything worth to my country".

But the years went by, to what he calls, in 'On Shakespeare', "the shame of slow-endeavouring art", and still he did not feel himself ready. 'Lycidas' is as much about being forced to write prematurely as it is about the premature death of his friend. In the 1650s, his political opponents (Salmasius and Alexander More) were able to touch him to the quick by describing him as a nobody, who has done nothing. He becomes touchy about his age, equivocating about how old he is, even claiming he looks younger than his years – a sign as much of anxiety as arrogance. The deep fear is that his "one talent, which is death to hide"[Sonnet 193] will prove to be nothing. His political service and his blindness are unavoidable causes of delay, but perhaps, he fears, no excuse. He has to convince himself that "They also serve who only stand and wait". [Sonnet 19] He was 58 when the first edition of *Paradise Lost* was published.◆

Opposite: Milton loathed William Marshall's engraving perhaps partly because he was so sensitive about his age (see opposite). He got his revenge by inducing Marshall, who knew no Greek, to engrave an inscription beneath, inviting friends to "laugh at the botching artist's mis-attempt". This was solemnly re-produced in the 1645 edition.

Ἀμαθεῖ γεγράφθαι χειρὶ τήνδε μὲν εἰκόνα
Φαίης τάχ' ἄν, πρὸς εἶδος αὐτοφυὲς βλέπων
Τὸν δ' ἐκτυπωτὸν οὐκ ἐπιγνόντες φίλοι
Γελᾶτε φαύλου δυσμίμημα ζωγράφου

W.M. sculp:

How does Milton portray the "counter-human" nature of evil?

True evil, by its very nature, lies beyond our understanding. When Primo Levi wrote about the Holocaust, he wrote that "we cannot, what is more we must not, understand what happened", because "to understand is almost to justify", and thereby to "contain it". What happened, Levi said, was non-human or "counter-human", and should remain incomprehensible. But this does not mean that we should become passive victims. Humanity, Levi urged, must always be vigilant. "We cannot understand it, but we can and must understand from where it springs, and we must be on our guard."

As a Puritan, Milton would approve of eternal moral vigilance, since "oft though wisdom wake, suspicion sleeps / At wisdom's gate". [III. 686-7] He would also agree that Satanic evil is beyond understanding, since in Christian theology evil is utterly negative, a mere privation of good (or God). Yet in *Paradise Lost* Milton nevertheless searches "from where it springs", in images exploring all that is most inexplicable and "counter-human" in that hinterland behind our acts of conscious choice.

Solomon, in all his wisdom, found

three things which are too wonderful for me; yea, four which I know not: the way of an eagle in the air; the way of a serpent upon a rock; the way of a ship in the midst of the sea; and the way of a man with a maid.

[Proverbs. 30. 18-19]

Satan in *Paradise Lost* is described in terms of all four of these 'unknowable' things, and all four merge and combine in his final assault on Eve. Ambiguous verbs are used in all these descriptions to sinister effect.

The hovering of an eagle in the air has already been touched on in discussing images of delay and contemplation: Eve's dream flight; Mulciber in freefall; those hovering clouds. At times, the way of the eagle in the air merges into the way of the ship in the midst of the sea. Satan, trying out his powers of flight in Book II,

...soars
Up to the fiery concave towering high.
As when far off at sea a fleet descried
Hangs in the clouds, by equinoctial winds
Close sailing from Bengala, or the isles
Of Ternate and Tidor, whence merchants bring
Their spicy drugs: they on the trading flood
Through the wide Ethipian to the Cape
Ply stemming nightly toward the pole.

[II. 634-43]

Satan is shown as like a bird of prey: "towering" describes the movement of a falcon or eagle, in the moment before it plummets to kill – like Shakespeare's "falcon towering in her height of pride" [*Macbeth* II. iv. 12]. This shifts into the metaphor of a fleet which is so far off that it seems like a mirage. Both images signal potential danger: birds of prey kill, ships may prove enemy forces. But all is still cloudy, not quite see-able. These are ships that "nightly" sail in darkness, carrying delusive "spicy" drugs; and though they seem at first to be gliding "on the flood" they turn out to be cunningly sailing against the wind and tides. (To "ply" is a nautical term for beating up against the wind, and "stemming" is making headway against a current.)

At the end of his quest, Satan's voyage is eased as he nears earth:

> *...Satan with less toil, and now with ease*
> *Wafts on the calmer wave by dubious light*
> *And like a weather-beaten vessel holds*
> *Gladly the port, though shrouds and tackle torn.*
> *[II. 1041-4]*

The ship comes in, in a tricky twilight of doubt and with another superbly ambiguous verb, "wafting", which serves for both flying and sailing. The "shrouds" (ship's rigging) are a reminder of the death this ship-of-doom will bring; and a "shroud" could also be a disguise. In this context, "vessel" may recall the Biblical "vessels of wrath fitted for destruction" [Romans ix. 22]: in Book IX, when Satan chooses the serpent as his disguise, the reptile is "fit vessel, fitted imp of fraud, in whom/ To enter, and his dark suggestions hide". [IX. 89] Milton's poetry is laden with "dark suggestions."

In Milton's day, setting sail upon the ocean was perilous. Sailors faced unknown hazards. The danger of storms was more real, but no less feared than the Leviathan and other monsters of the deep; and when Satan is described as a sea-faring explorer, we can recognise his courage. His epic quest through Chaos, indeed, echoes the heroic voyage of classical sea-faring heroes. He is "beset" like Jason navigating "the jostling rocks", or like Odysseus steering between Scylla and Charybdis. [II. 1016-20] Satan, however, is more often described as the treacherous and endangering ship than the skilful and endangered pilot.

If Milton's ship-metaphors seem particularly fraught, it is worth remembering that in 1637 one of his friends, Edward King, was drowned at sea. Milton's elegy for his dead friend, *Lycidas,* contains a powerful image of a treacherous ship:

> *...that fatal and perfidious bark*
> *Built in the eclipse, and rigged with curses dark...*
> *[100-1]*

Just as the way of the eagle merges into the way of

the ship, so, in the final temptation of Eve in Book IX, the way of the ship merges into the way of the serpent on the rock. Satan, approaching Eve, is given a linguistically deceptive and shimmering slither, which is made to seem simultaneously straight and circling, upright and wave-like.

So spake the enemy of mankind...
...and toward Eve
Addressed his way, not with indented wave,
Prone on the ground, as since, but on his rear,
Circular base of rising folds, that towered
Fold above fold a surging maze, his head
Crested aloft, and carbuncle his eyes;
With burnished neck of verdant gold, erect
Amidst his circling spires, that on the grass
Floated redundant...

[IX. 495-503]

The serpent seems to float on waves of itself. The description is charged with danger: there is the maze or labyrinth, a symbol of error, in which it is easy to get lost. There are also towers and (apparently) spires, emblems throughout *Paradise Lost* of pride, aspiration, and the idolatrous "high places" of the Bible. Satan is "like a tower" [I. 591];

Opposite: The Fall, *by Hugo van der Goes (c.1440-1482), an example of how artists tried to solve the problem of what the serpent looked like before it went on its belly. The sword-like leaves of the iris, pointing at Eve's womb, are traditional iconographic symbols of suffering, suggesting the post-fall pains of childbirth, inflicted by God's curse. The abalone shell - in Latin a "sea-ear" - suggests the specifically aural nature of Eve's temptation*

there is the presumptuous tower of Babel [XII. 44]; the "proud towers" of the rebel angels [V. 907]; and though there are towers in heaven, their architect, Mulciber, falls, "nor aught availed him now to have built in heaven high towers". [I. 749] Spires in Milton's poetry have a gilded allure: they are "glistering" [III. 550], or, in *Paradise Regained,* "glittering" and "golden" [*Paradise Regained* IV. 54 and 548]. In this passage, however, the towers are a linguistic illusion: "spires" here means "writhing spirals". Satan shifts shape in the mind of the reader who realises this.

Linguistic shape-shifting merges into fables of snaky metamorphosis and seduction, and these, in their turn, merge into the way of the ship in the midst of the sea, sailing with cunning shifts. Satan in serpent form is more attractive even than Jove, when he became a snake to seduce Olympias,

...who bore
Scipio the height of Rome. With tract oblique
At first, as one who sought access, but feared
To interrupt, sidelong he works his way.
As when a ship by skilful steersman wrought
Nigh river's mouth or foreland, where the wind
Veers oft, as oft so steers, and shifts her sail;
So varied he...

[IX. 509-516]

Milton creates a brilliant visual pattern here. The

letters at the start of the first five lines spell out 'SATAN', reading "sidelong" and with "tract oblique". It is an extraordinary effect for a blind man to imagine and construct. Despite the eternal vigilance of Miltonic critics, this acrostic was not spotted until 1977.

How do Milton's politics affect his portrayal of choice?

One of the many images of sinister, hovering flux in *Paradise Lost* is the comparison of the devils to a "pitchy cloud / Of locusts, warping on the eastern wind". [I. 340-1] "Warping" is another of Milton's superbly ambiguous, sinister verbs: it means 'floating in the air', but there is the obvious suggestion of perverting or distorting – though here the devils are warping only themselves. A cloud of swirling insects, morphing like a single organism, makes a superb image for a mind mysteriously self-warping towards a decision. In *Paradise Lost*, however, this image has a political as well as a psychological dimension. Locusts are, for Solomon, another 'unknowable' mystery, because "the locusts have no king ,yet they go forth all of them by bands". (Proverbs 30. 27)

This is a metaphor for evil which might seem strange, since Milton was and remained an unrepentant republican, who had helped to dethrone and behead the King of England. When the original censor – the Archbishop of Canterbury's chaplain, Thomas Tomkyns – was handed the first edition of *Paradise Lost* in 1667, the young royalist clergyman may well have been surprised. God is made an absolute monarch, "Heaven's perpetual King" [I. 131]; and the devils debate in an infernal Parliament, spouting republican sentiments.

This is not inconsistency on Milton's part. He always asserted that according to 'natural law' the only just form of rule was rule by the worthiest, wisest and best. God, of course, on these criteria, must be the worthiest to rule. He is perfectly wise, and absolutely good, and so perfectly fit to be an absolute monarch.

Milton did not, however, believe in divine right for earthly kings – that doctrine, based on the text "the powers that be are ordained of God" [Romans 8. 1], which held that all rulers are sanctioned by God, and all rebellion therefore sinful as well as unlawful. Milton argued that a king or magistrate ruled not by divine right, but under an implicit contract with his people to govern in their best interests. If he broke that contract, becoming a tyrant, he could be deposed.

Milton was a passionate champion of liberty, but he never conflated it with equality. "No man who knows aught, can be so stupid to deny that all men naturally were born free," he asserts ringingly in *The Tenure of Kings and Magistrates*; yet, it turns out, some men are freer than others. "None can love freedom heartily, but good men; the rest love not freedom, but licence." Only the virtuous possess the inner freedom upon which true liberty depends. Milton was never a democrat, and his insistence on rule by the worthiest only substitutes a moral and spiritual aristocracy for a hereditary one.

An idealist, he failed to foresee the difficulties in finding an agreed form of virtue-based government to replace the monarchy. It proved impossible to decide who was 'worthiest' to rule – particularly if only the worthy were qualified to decide who was worthy. Mere logic could not find it out; only "right reason", which is reason rectified by grace. "True liberty... always with right reason dwells / Twinned" [XII. 83-5]; but only right reason knows what right reason is.

Milton's political pamphlets during the course of the revolution reflect his mounting desperation as the nation becomes, in his view, progressively morally disenfranchised. Though he increasingly insists on the inclusive Arminian view that sufficient grace is available to all men, he also insists that true inner liberty has been achieved only by a few. And then, as the pamphlets go on, by fewer and then fewer still, until he sees himself as a solitary voice crying in the wilderness.

In the lonely years after the Restoration, he had ample time to think how difficult it is for a nation to choose right.

How is Milton's feeling of personal betrayal reflected in *Paradise Lost*?

Milton felt betrayed by the people of England, who had proved themselves to be only a "rabble" and not a true "Nation". But he also felt that the people had been betrayed by leaders who had "misguided and abused" them, including those on his own side who had wasted a God-given opportunity to build a New Jerusalem in England.

Both betrayals are reflected in *Paradise Lost*, and in Milton's preoccupation with the ways in which false choices are made. Individual choice is analogous to that of a nation, since in times of decision, as Shakespeare put it,

The genius and the mortal instruments
Are then in council; and the state of man,
Like to a little kingdom, suffers then
The nature of an insurrection.
[Julius Caesar, II. i. 66-9]

In Book II, Satan stands on the brink of a place of

anarchy and perpetual civil war, suffering "the nature of an insurrection". This "hoary deep" is the kingdom of "eldest Night" and "Chaos", where the very atoms of matter are in perpetual flux:

For Hot, Cold, Moist, Dry, four champions fierce
Strive here for mastery, and to battle bring
Their embryon atoms; they around the flag
Of each his faction, in their several clans
Light-armed or heavy, sharp, smooth, swift or slow,
Swarm populous, unnumbered as the sands
Or Barca or Cyrene's torrid soil,
Levied to side with warring winds, and poise
Their lighter wings. To whom these most adhere
He rules a moment; Chaos umpire sits,
And by decision more embroils the fray
By which he reigns; next him high arbiter
Chance governs all.

[II. 898-910]

It is an image of mass-decision-making, where numerical might is right: raw democracy, in other words, which is akin to civil war. The armies that rally round the flags of their factions are "levied", which can mean both 'enlisted' and 'lifted up'. This is another image of hovering, and of insect-like crowds that "swarm populous". Milton feared the levity of the masses: "the giddy favour of a mutining rout is as dangerous as their fury". He would never have accepted a political system in which elections are decided by "floating voters". This image of a seething flux of indecision comes specifically at the moment when, in the narrative, Satan is hesitating on the brink of the void (another moment of delay, brilliantly rendered):

> *...Into this wild abyss,*
> *The womb of nature and perhaps her grave...*
> *Into this wild abyss the wary fiend*
> *Stood on the brink of hell and looked a while*
> *Pondering his voyage...*
>
> *[II. 910-19]*

The critic and editor Alistair Fowler comments on

> a fine passage of mimetic syntax. The lack of any continuation at all after the first 'Into this wild abyss' (l. 910), and the lack of the expected verb of motion after the second, render the repeated hesitations of the wary fiend: when we are fully prepared for him to leap or plunge, he stands.

The teeming abyss into which Satan is about to leap is the emptiness of a universe without God, but also the "mutining rout" within himself. Ancient Greek philosophers like Democritus and Lucretius had envisaged a deterministic universe made up of randomly colliding atoms, governed by only a spontaneous deviation (*clinamen*) from their trajectory. Christian commentators conflated this with the Biblical account of an uncreated universe "without form and void". [Genesis 1. 2] God created order, coherence and meaning out of "his dark materials" [II. 916]: this "hoary deep", then, is a description of those empty, dark and godless places where the Almighty does not exercise his creative power.

For God, this is a matter of choice. He reaches everywhere, and fills "infinitude, nor vacuous the space"; but he may, he asserts,

...uncircumscribed my self retire
And put not forth my goodness, which is free
To act or not, necessity and chance
Approach not me, and what I will is fate.
[VII. 169-73]

As a personal statement, the last lines have a boastful ring: God sounds unfortunately like W.H. Henley in his stirring poem, 'Invictus' ("I am the master of my fate;/ I am the captain of my soul"). As a theological statement, however, it is important. "Necessity and chance" rule in the kingdom of old Night, but only because God permits it: this is why Satan's quest through the abyss is shown to be saved from failure by a "chance" gust of wind, which on a psychological level is a random, violent, instinctive urge. "Some tumultuous cloud/Instinct with fire" [II. 925-7] blows him upwards: Satan is like Gide's Lafcadio, whose every impulse is an arbitrary one.

Since evil is an absence of good, St Augustine remarks that describing its inception is as impossible as "seeing darkness, or hearing silence". But Milton's poetry dares the impossible. Famously, he evokes "darkness visible"; less notoriously, in the abyss his hesitating Devil is battered by the white noise of heard silence: "Nor was his ear less pealed / With noises loud and ruinous..." No source is given for this tumult, which is a ringing in his ears, as when a

...universal hubbub wild
Of stunning sounds and voices all confused
Borne through the hollow dark assaults his ear...
[II. 951]

This sound seems 'born' out of the hollow dark, as well as borne through it: a many-voiced but meaningless sound actually created by empty space, like tinnitus in the hollow dark of an ear-drum. Milton's abyss is, in another oxymoron, crowd-filled emptiness.

Hell is "hollow": "the hollow deep"[I. 314], the "hollow abyss"[II. 518], echoing with "sonorous metal blowing martial sounds"[I. 540], where the tautology of "sonorous sounds" neatly suggests the self-convincing nature of devilish rhetoric. The fiend can "invade vacant possession" [XI. 103], and especially the emptiness in crowds.

In the council in Hell, rhetoric sways devils who are a crowd of "hollow men, behaving as the wind behaves", in T.S.Eliot's phrase. They have been listening too long to speeches, and in the aftermath of Mammon's address,

...such murmur filled
The assembly, as when hollow rocks retain
The sound of blustering winds, which all night long
Had roused the sea, now with hoarse cadence lull
Sea-faring men o'er-watched, whose bark by chance
Or pinnace anchors in a craggy bay
After the tempest.

[II. 284-9]

There is another crowd image in *Paradise Lost* which strongly suggests Milton's political frustrations, as well as being psychologically searching. Swarming or "populous" insects recur in the image of the bee-hive in Book I. Bees are an ambiguous insect for Milton to employ, since they were traditionally emblems of good monarchical rule. (Ants, Milton's "parsimonious emmet" [VII. 485], traditionally embodied republican virtues.) In one of his pamphlets, Milton argued against the notion that the loyalty of bees to their monarch proves that there is a 'natural law' underlying kingship.

In *Paradise Lost*, Milton neatly side-steps the

question of what a natural apian constitution might be. He shows the devils in hell as bees that have not yet formed a colony and made up their collective mind.

This is one of the similes in *Paradise Lost* which might be described as Homeric, comparing large things to small. It seems, despite the ominously serpentine "hiss of rustling wings", to be inappropriately homely and cheerful:

> *...As bees*
> *Pour forth their populous youth about the hive*
> *In clusters; they among fresh dews and flowers*
> *Fly to and fro, or on the smoothed plank,*
> *The suburb of their straw-built citadel,*
> *New-rubbed with balm, expatiate and confer*
> *Their state...*
>
> *[I. 768-775]*

This is evidently a new and uninhabited bee-hive, since the bee-keeper has rubbed the ramp with sweet-smelling syrup to tempt the swarm inside (a common bee-keeping practice). But the bees are passing up a heaven-sent opportunity. Everything has been made ready for them to create their own community: the plank has even been anointed with sacred "balm" and "smoothed" – as God makes "the rough places smooth" to prepare the way for a new Jerusalem. [Isaiah 44.2; Luke 3.

Opposite: 1808 illustration by William Blake showing Adam and Eve watched by Satan holding a serpent

5] Yet the bees just buzz about: they "expatiate and confer". "Expatiate", meaning both wandering about and expounding arguments, is a bitter description of time-wasting discussions.

Milton had lived through a time of intense ideological debate, political and theological. All those revolutionary speeches, discussions and sermons, all those Putney debates, all those projections of models for a new society – all had come to nothing. The bees "confer", but as they talk the sense of "confer" shifts, and it turns out they are talking away their chances of power; they "confer their state". Their cheerfulness, it turns out, is another example of an inappropriate holiday mood. These bees are neither quite the masses nor their leaders: they are a swarm of would-be leaders – student politicians, perhaps.

In the Council in Hell, Milton portrays the powerful politicians who misled the people. The parade of arguments by Moloch, Belial, Mammon and Beelzebub is a fierce and acute satire upon political types, but it is important to realise that even these high-ranking devils turn out to have little power.

All of the great debates in Book I are effectively stage-managed by Satan, who dominates this mass rally. The Council in Hell is a perverted parody of true republicanism. Even before the meeting is called, Satan has become a like a "sultan" [I. 348], an oriental despot – and before the devils have any

Satan on his Throne: *illustration by John Martin, (1789-1854), published 1858*

chance to vote on a leader, he is already exalted "high on a throne of royal state". [II. 1]

When Mammon has managed to sway the masses of "hollow men", so that "the popular vote / Inclines" towards peace, and Beelzebub rises to counter-act his counsel, it is clear that in his proposal to corrupt mankind he is in fact 'fronting' Satan's plan. The strategy was actually "first devised / By Satan". [I. 379-80]

The devils vote "with full assent" to the scheme, but Beelzebub then presents it in such a way that the devils in practice have no choice. He vividly stresses the dangers of the quest to find Paradise:

But first whom shall we send
In search of this new world, whom shall we find

Sufficient? Who shall tempt with wandering feet
The dark, unbottomed infinite abyss
And through the palpable obscure find out
His uncouth way, or spread his airy flight
Upborn with indefatigable wings
Over the vast abrupt...

[II. 402-9]

It is little wonder that there is only one volunteer. The devils, Beelzebub says, will have to be "choice in their suffrage" – (i.e. discriminating in their election), but this is an election with only one candidate. Satan, who offers himself "with

SATAN, CROMWELL AND THE REPUBLICAN CROWN

Some of the charge for this scene must come from the ambiguities of Milton's own political life as an apologist for Cromwell. By the end of the Revolution, Milton found himself forced by circumstances to argue that Cromwell was, in such turbulent times, the single "man most fit to rule". Like many an idealist before and since, Milton, the champion of personal liberty, ended up supporting a military dictatorship, at least as a temporary measure. He must have known he was arguing from "necessity, / The tyrant's plea". [IV. 394]

Cromwell was formally offered the crown of England by a delegation of MPs in 1657. After uncomfortably long deliberation, he turned it down. He was installed as Lord Protector instead, but monarchal pride / Conscious of highest worth" [II. 249], at the same time accepts a kingship which no one has ever formally offered him, and whose trappings he has in any event already appropriated:

...Wherefore do I assume
These royalties, and not refuse to reign..
[I. 450-1]

Satan is arguing that since he is the only one who dares to execute the plan, he is the worthiest to rule – which is true, though only if courage is the chief criterion of merit.

with many of the trappings of royal state (throne, sceptre, purple robes, coach of state; even a Coronation oath) – dangerous stuff, in republican eyes.

This is not, of course, to claim that Satan is intended to represent Cromwell – unlike Satan, Cromwell refused the Crown. But Satan in his rise "to that bad eminence" [II. 6] surely offers a perverted version of Cromwellianism. Milton saw the dangers inherent in the increasingly absolute powers of the Protectorate, and in his pamphlets took it upon himself to warn Cromwell of the threats to Cromwell's character, as well as to the state. Cromwell, Milton cautioned, might become "captivated" by the title of king, and find the temptations inherent in power would "search [him] wholly and intimately".

Satan exemplifies Milton's fears for the republican ideal. Driven by greed for unshared glory and sole power, he is shown in the course of *Paradise Lost* to be increasingly corrupted as well as corrupting.◆

How does Milton portray a good decision?

If crowds in *Paradise Lost* are corruptible, this does not mean they are themselves evil. Milton is fascinated by the dynamics of what we now call crowd psychology: the ways in which people act and react differently when they are in a crowd. Crowds generate emotion: the experience of attending a live football match is different from watching the same event on television at home. One can lose a sense of oneself in a crowd – which can be exhilarating, but is also disturbing. If the prevailing *clinamen* (or inclination) of a crowd is panic, or even malice, as in a Nazi mass-rally, it is all too easy to be swept along.

There is, however, one interesting image in *Paradise Lost* that explores a *good* resolution in terms of mass-decision-making, featuring a crowd of unfallen angels rather than devils. It is fascinatingly ambiguous – a borderline case, perhaps because it is taking place on the borders of consciousness.

In Book IV, Satan takes the form of a toad to squat by the sleeping Eve and "taint" her imagination by whispering in her ear. (He is, we discover in the next book, infecting her with the dream of flying.) He is interrupted by the angelic guard, and is taken, in his own shape, to answer to Gabriel. There is a typically Miltonic stand-off

Ithuriel and Zephon, *by Gustave Doré (1832 – 1883). The spirits, Ithuriel and Zephon, fly to keep watch over Adam and Eve. Book IV.*

TEN FACTS ABOUT MILTON AND *PARADISE LOST*

1.

Milton is our greatest poetic neologist (coiner of new words), according to Professor Gavin Alexander. Alexander finds 630 words whose first-time use is credited to Milton by the *Oxford English Dictionary*. Shakespeare trails in fourth with 229. Some are demanded by Milton's subject matter (*pandemonium; arch-fiend; Satanic, cherubic; adamantean*). 135 begin with the prefix un- ; suggesting the important of negatives in describing what is otherwise (another coinage) unaccountable. Many of them prove that Milton was radically stretching our awareness of the human mind: *sensuous, love-lorn, besottedly, ecstatic, exhilarating, enjoyable, jubilant, awe-struck, hot-headed, loquacious, impassive, depravity, self-delusion*... The list is *terrific; stunning*.

2.

One of Milton's neologisms in *Paradise Lost* was to apply the word "space" to interstellar expanses. He imagines the possibility of "other worlds" and life on other planets. [III. 566; VIII. 144-152] His interest was scientific. In 1638 he visited Galileo in prison, when the 'heretical' astronomer was 78, and as blind as Milton would become.

3.

Milton began to lose his sight when he was 36. His

right eye failed first, then his left. He was blind by 44, seeing the world as "ashy-grey". Glaucoma has been suggested as the cause.

In an attempt to save his second eye, Milton was treated with "issues and setons" i.e. a red-hot needle was thrust through the skin in his neck, and a thread impregnated with white of egg and oil of roses drawn through it, keeping the wounds open and oozing to 'draw the humours from the face'.

4.

Milton, who in *Areopagitica* famously pleaded for freedom of speech, later found himself working as a government censor. In 1649, he became the Secretary for Foreign Tongues, drafting documents into Latin for Cromwell's Council of State. But this job was bundled up with a post as 'Licenser', set up under the 1649 Press Act to clamp down on anti-government pamphlets.

5.

Around 1658, the three best poets of the age – Milton, Marvell and John Dryden – were all employed as bureaucrats by Cromwell's regime.

6.

In June 1660 Milton was nearly the 'twentieth man' on a Commons hit-list. Twenty names of notable non-regicides (supporters who had not actually signed the King's death warrant) were considered for exclusion from the Act of Indemnity and Oblivion, which offered a general pardon. Milton's name was mooted as the last on the list. The poet Andrew Marvell, MP for Hull, campaigned "vigorously" on his behalf. Milton escaped exclusion; but he was imprisoned, and forced to pay £150 in 'fees'.

7.

Milton was paid only £5 for the first edition of *Paradise Lost* (1667). This seems like the world's worst book deal. But Milton was more canny than this seems. The agreement between him and his publisher is the earliest surviving publishing contract; and shows that Milton had invented an early form of royalties. Samuel Simmons agreed to pay Milton £5 for the first edition, which was capped at 1,500 copies; but a further £5 for each of the subsequent three editions, payable each time after the sale of 1,300 copies: £20 was then a good going rate – and far more than any publisher would be willing to pay up front for a work by a known supporter of regicide. But *Paradise Lost* sold slowly, and only one more edition (1674) was published before Milton's death.

8.

Milton's relations with his three daughters by his first wife, Mary, were strained. He insisted that Ann, Mary and Deborah should read to him in Hebrew, Syriac, Greek, Latin, Italian, Spanish, and French, all of which they had to pronounce "exactly", "without understanding one word." As Milton's nephew remarked, "this must needs be a trial of patience, almost beyond endurance." The sisters took their revenge by fiddling the household accounts, and stealing his books to sell. Milton left them out of his will.

9.

Milton died of "a fit of gout".

10.

The influence of *Paradise Lost* upon other writers would fill many volumes. Dryden made a play of it, *The State of Innocence*; Pope parodied it (*The Rape of the Lock*; and *The Dunciad*). Every major Romantic poet worshipped Milton. Blake (who read Book IV of *Paradise Lost* in the nude, in the garden with his wife) saw and talked with Milton in his visions. Byron's alienated and darkly passionate heroes are cast in Satanic mould. Keats gave up his epic poem *Hyperion* because the influence of Milton was too strong. Shelley, who wrote *Milton's Spirit*, read *Paradise Lost* aloud to his wife, Mary – who wrote *Frankenstein*, an extraordinary re-invention of the myth of creation. *Paradise Lost* provides the epigraph to *Frankenstein*, and is the monster's favourite reading: his vocabulary is a far cry from Boris Karloff. C.S Lewis re-wrote *Paradise Lost* as sci-fi, with a happy ending for a green alien Eve, which is not an improvement (*Perelandra*).

between the two, with argument and lengthy counter-argument: if one feels this intolerably delays the action, Milton characteristically reinforces this impression with a subliminal pun: "Satan alarmed / Collecting all his might dilated stood..." "Dilated" suggests physical swelling – morally toad-like still, since toads puff themselves up in times of danger – but 'to dilate' could also mean 'to delay, defer or extend'. And Milton, again as usual, makes his narrative even more dilatory by inserting an extended simile which even Christopher Ricks describes as "beautiful, but digressive". Like that moment when W.H.Auden's "crowds upon the pavement/ Were fields of harvest wheat", the angels are depersonalised:

While thus he spake, the angelic squadron bright
Turned fiery red, sharpening in mooned horns
Their phalanx, and began to hem him round
With ported spears, as thick as when a field
Of Ceres ripe for harvest waving bends
Her bearded grove of ears, which way the wind
Sways them; the careful ploughman doubting stands
Lest on the threshing floor his hopeful sheaves
Prove chaff.

[IV. 9777-985]

Empson objects that "if God the sower is the ploughman, then he is anxious", which would reveals that he is not omnipotent. Nor can Satan be the one feeling doubt, since he is shown in the next line to be standing "on the other side".

But though an allusion to the final Day of Judgment is certainly intended, this is primarily an image of human choice and human judgment, which will be judged by God on the Last Day. In the medieval poem, *Piers Plowman*, Piers represents the human soul, labouring to become Christ-like; here, too, the humble ploughman is an image of everyday humanity.

The angels are represented in a state of indecision, their spears "ported" – which is a halfway position between being shouldered and levelled at the enemy. And in this state, the rippling of the angelic field of corn is beautifully but almost devilishly mysterious: they are bending their "ears", as though listening to unknown rumours, and swayed by sourceless "winds".

The winds that shake this barley could be good. The operation of the Holy Spirit was often compared to a "rushing mighty wind" (Acts, 2.2). But Milton, who had lived through a time of Puritan revolution, knew the dangers of 'enthusiasm' – the often crazed belief in personal inspiration by the inrushing of the Holy Spirit. In *Paradise Lost,* winds are usually associated with strong and dangerous passions: they are "violent" [III. 487], "fierce" [I. 235], "blustering" [II. 286], "warring" [II. 905], "impetuous" [4. 560], "envious" [XI. 15], "subterranean" [I. 231], "furious" [III. 213]... No wonder this ploughman is "careful". In this image, the winds are neither good nor bad, but properly mysterious – as indeed are the operations of the Holy Spirit in the Bible: "The wind bloweth where it listeth, and thou hearest the sound thereof, but canst not tell whence it cometh, and whither it goeth..." [John 3.8]

If this is an image of counter-logical virtuous impulses, this may be because it reflects what is happening in Eve's dreaming mind. Her dreamt revulsion to temptation was instinctive. Mere fideism is only precariously good; and she

ABDIEL'S HEROISM

An unambiguous hero in *Paradise Lost,* who might almost be described as the moral centre of the poem, even though he has only a walk-on part, is Abdiel in Book V. Abdiel is the lone angel who stands firm against the ugly mood of the crowd of Satanic supporters, and refuses to join with Satan. Mass psychology here is represented in familiar Miltonic imagery: the applause of the "infinite host" is another "hoarse murmur", like "the sound of waters deep" [V. 872-3]; Satanic influence spreads like "contagion". [V. 880] Abdiel resists. He is a form of good rebel; a virtuous individual in a corrupt society, which was doubtless how Milton the republican, still holding bravely to what he called "the Good Old Cause", thought of himself in the Restoration:

anyway can take no true, "approved" decision in her sleep.

This sense of precariousness prevents the image of the golden balance which ends the stand-off in Book IV becoming clichéd as an image for a good decision. Even when the decision is being taken by "the eternal", and the scales are as stable as possible, it is not felt to be easy. God's golden scales are the instrument with which he weighed "all things" at creation. In his overview of the "pendulous round earth" he takes in at one comprehensive glance "all events, / Battles and realms" throughout all history – and, presumably,

---

Among the faithless,
faithful only he;
Among innumerable
false, unmoved,
Unshaken, unseduced,
unterrified,
His loyalty he kept, his love,
his zeal;
Nor number, nor example
with him wrought
To swerve from truth, or
change his constant mind
Though single.
[V. 897-903]

Abdiel, it is worth noting, is the only character who soliloquizes when taking a good decision. Satan and Abdiel get the chance to put each other to the test again, in the battle in heaven. "On the rough edge of battle ere it joined", Abdiel "thus his own undaunted heart explores," "pondering" aloud. But the opening of his speech gives the clue as to why he can do so: "O heaven!" he begins. [VI. 113-4] Abdiel is addressing God, rather than – or as well as – himself; his sense of selfhood remains firm, precisely because he is "trusting in the almighty's aid", and not in his own powers.◆

decides that the ultimate outcome will be "happier far" if Adam and Eve are tested, even if they do fall. It is an image of all possible considerations weighed up and held in suspension.

Because this is God, however, it is not an image of delay. God's decision is "quick". God indeed never delays: "immediate are the acts of God, more swift / Than time or motion". [VII. 176-7] He may "suspend" his punishments [VI. 692], to allow for sinners to harden their hearts, like Satan, or repent, like Adam and Eve; but his actual verdict is instant: "without delay/ To judgment he proceeded on the accused..."[X. 163-4]

God, of course, has the advantage of foreknowledge. Human beings have to do the best they can, with past, present, and "collected" anticipation. God scrupulously (a scruple, of course is literally a tiny weight) refuses to interfere with the balance of man's choice: he will not

> *...touch with lightest moment of impulse*
> *His free will, to her own inclining left*
> *In even scale...*
>
> *[X. 45-7]*

But left to itself, the mind has become both weigher and the thing weighed, and the internal dynamics that could tip the scale are baffling. The will is left "to her own inclining", but the will *is* the inclination of the soul. The self-reflexive nature of

Milton's image suggests the baffling nature of free will, considered in itself. As Dr Johnson remarked, after reading a book that convincingly refuted Arminianism, "All theory is against the freedom of the will, all experience for it".

We know, of course, what Milton believes should weigh in the balance. "Amor meus, pondus meum", as St Augustine puts it: "my love is my weight". The love of God is the gravitational urge that should centre one's whole soul – if it is not to be light, giddy, "weighed in the balance and found wanting"; and a wise ruler uses it to ballast a "giddy, vicious and ungrounded people". But Milton's belief in the importance of both the love of God and of free will never leads him to over-simplification; instead, he uses all the riches of his poetry to show that it is never easy to be a true ruler, even – or indeed particularly – over one's own soul.

How does Milton use rhetoric to suggest the counter-logical nature of evil?

The most potent counter-logical force in *Paradise Lost* is language itself; significantly, the last elaborate metaphor describing Satan as he approaches Eve compares him to a classical orator.

Milton both exulted in and distrusted the powers of oratory. He was educated in a culture dominated by the study of rhetoric; but the rhetorically-based curriculum of Renaissance schoolboys and university students could encourage brilliant cynicism. Students were trained to debate on any side of an argument, and to construct rhetorical paradoxes. A rhetorical paradox was a set-piece exercise arguing as perversely as possible against received or orthodox opinion: Donne's prose pieces, "A Defence of Woman's Inconstancy", or "That the Gifts of the Body are Better than those of the Minde" are examples, as is his poem "The Flea", with its brilliantly perverse praise of the contemptible.

But writers like Donne and Milton who had been schooled this way knew that language was infinitely flexible, and could be infinitely manipulative as well as infinitely rich. The true danger of being a brilliant rhetorician is like that of being a superb actor. One may convince not just others, but even oneself – like Conrad's Mr Kurtz in *The Heart of Darkness*, who "could get himself to believe anything – anything".

Milton is fascinated by the dark arts of oratory. A trained orator can gain a mysterious ascendency over his audience even before he opens his mouth, and *Paradise Lost* captures the phenomenon of charisma – the potentially sinister allure of the public speaker. Beelzebub is Satan's right hand man and 'spin-doctor' – and when he stands up to speak in council, "with grave/ Aspect he rose... [II. 300-1] There is a pun in "aspect", which gives the look of his face the astrological influence of a rising star ("aspect" is another term from astronomy). He can effortlessly command an audience:

> *...his look*
> *Drew audience and attention still as night*
> *Or summer's noontide air...*
>
> *[II. 307-9]*

Noon, and midnight, are always the hours of peak temptation in Milton's poetry; and the syntax makes it impossible to tell whether it is Beelzebub's "look" or his audience that is compellingly still, so much does the one command the other.

The Council in Hell offers all kinds of dubious rhetoric. Satan opens the Grand Consult, appealing, like a true lawyer-politician, to false precedent. The master of the dodgy dossier, he starts with the claims of the devils, addressing them by their forfeited heavenly titles as "Powers and dominions, deities of heaven", and asserting that since hell cannot hold "immortal vigour", they will be able to reascend as "Celestial virtues rising". [II. 12-15] But these devils are neither heavenly nor virtuous. Satan is using titles as if they convey inalienable power – as if they express hereditary rights, rather than intrinsic merit.

Intrinsic merit, however, is exactly what he claims for himself:

> *Me though just right, and the fixed laws of heaven*
> *Did first create your leader, next free choice,*
> *With what besides, in counsel or in fight,*
> *Hath been achieved in merit...*
>
> *[II. 18-21]*

What exactly are the "fixed laws of heaven" that sanction a devil taking charge? And how do "fixed laws" square with "free choice"? Milton had lived through the Civil War, and knew from bitter experience the fragility of claims to rule based upon self-asserted worth. There is in *Paradise Lost* both the thinnest of lines and a "gulf profound" between the Arminian concept of "self-esteem, grounded on just and right" [VIII. 572], and Satanic pride. Satan's speech ends with a blatant rhetorical paradox – a passage of pure Donne-like bravado, arguing that hell is a better place than heaven. In hell, there is no envy, and so there is "union, and firm faith, and firm accord, / More than can be in heaven". [II. 36-7] But what envy is there in heaven, now Satan has been expelled?

After Satan, the lawyer-politician, comes Moloch, the bluff soldier, and the 'hawk' of this War Council. He professes to know no "wiles", and never discusses whether there is any justification for his proposed war. He sees God only as "the torturer". His crude eagerness to attack leads him into obvious exaggeration – and self-contradiction.

He starts by picturing an assault on heaven which will "force resistless way" [II. 63], and claims that "the ascent is easy then" [II. 81] – an obvious untruth – then contradicts himself by admitting God's throne to be "inaccessible". [II. 104]

Moloch's apparent confidence turns out to be the counsel of despair, or of a suicide-bomber: nothing can make their present situation worse, so annihilation would be a welcome release. He urges the devils to attack and die, even as he admits that this is only a futile gesture: "perpetual" waves of attackers will merely "disturb his heaven", "which if not victory is yet revenge". [II. 100-5] A barren ethos.

The next speaker is Belial, whose rhetoric is more plausible: "his tongue/ Dropt manna, and could make the worse appear/ The better reason." [II. 112-4] He points out that Moloch "grounds his courage on despair"; but his own plans are based upon facile optimism. Belial is the laissez-faire politician, whose apparent pragmatism and talk of peace masks laziness and moral cowardice. Again, it is the self-contradictions that are most telling. Belial starts by arguing that things could easily get worse, and ends by arguing that they might get better, but seems prepared to let "chance" determine whether they do. [II. 222]

Mammon, the next speaker, is more energetic. He is like a capitalist, arguing that the situation should be exploited, especially the mineral resources; and though he urges self-improvement, it is only within thoroughly debased limits. He too deploys republican rhetoric, professing to value "hard liberty before the easy yoke / Of servile pomp". This is obviously a mere rhetorical flourish – particularly since by describing by God's "yoke" as "easy" Mammon actually contradicts his own earlier argument that God rules by intolerably "strict laws". [II. 256 and 241] He is, of course, implicitly rejecting Christianity, while not even substituting high-minded Roman values. He proposes to build an empire, but one which is made up entirely of ersatz "magnificence" – which is true "servile Pomp". The light and glory of heaven is to be imitated by the glitter of gold. "What can heaven show more?" Mammon asks, rhetorically: he, apparently, can see no difference between the light of virtue and mere bling.

How does Satan use rhetoric to beguile Eve?

The self-contradictions of these politician-devils are evident. Satan, the Great Deceiver, is more accomplished. When in Book IX he shimmers towards Eve in serpent form, his "varied" approach "shifts" and "veers" [515-6]; and so does his beguiling rhetoric.

He begins, as he did in the dream-temptation, by exploiting the rhetoric of courtly love poetry. He plays the part of a Cavalier love-poet, who flatters his mistress by praising her as a goddess – in order, of course, to seduce her. Between two courtly lovers who both know the rules of the game, this is one thing; but Milton represents Satan as a city sophisticate, " long in populous city pent", "issuing forth" to the unspoiled countryside for a holiday, and encountering there an innocent "fair virgin". [IX. 445-451]

Typically, however, Milton suggests "wily subtleties and refluxes" within this unequal encounter. The city-dweller genuinely "conceives delight" in both the countryside and the country girl – "What pleasing seemed, for her now pleases more" – and the innocence which is part of her attraction has its own powers. Satan "took pleasure" in the sight of Eve, and

Her graceful innocence, her every air
Of gesture or least action overawed
His malice, and with rapine sweet bereaved
His fierceness of the fierce intent he brought...
[IX. 459-462]

For a moment, there seems the possibility that innocence will be its own protection; but Satan's genuine admiration only brings a reflux of envy at "pleasure not for him ordained". When he says he will destroy "all pleasure... Save what is in destroying" [IX. 477-79], he is destroying not just the pleasures of others, because he cannot share them, but even what momentarily gave *him* pleasure – which is just what a seducer does, when he corrupts the very innocence that attracted him. Satan, as always, is shown to be self-destructive in his destructiveness.

Satan's initial admiration is sincere; his impulses to evil have to be whipped up again by his own rhetoric:

> *Fierce hate he recollects, and all his thoughts*
> *Of mischief, gratulating, thus excites...*
> *[IX. 471-2]*

But that residue of admiration gives Satan's manipulative wooing of Eve its power. Even to himself, Satan finds Eve "fair, divinely fair, fit love for gods" [IX. 489]; and this becomes the keynote of his cynical seduction. Sincere insincerity is the most dangerous of weapons.

Satan's perverted love-poem rings brilliant changes on tropes, or lyrical forms, which would be near-clichés to Milton's audience, though to poor Eve, of course, they seem entirely new. His way of shifting the meanings of words is particularly adroit.

Wonder not, sovereign mistress, if perhaps
Thou canst, who art sole wonder, much less arm
Thy looks the heaven of mildness, with disdain...
[IX. 532]

If Eve had stopped to "wonder" at why a serpent was speaking to her, she might have become suspicious. Satan smoothly shifts the wonder from verb to noun, to suggest flatteringly that Eve herself should be the only proper object of (male) admiration. And Eve, a queen in the first line, is already becoming like a goddess in the third, ruling in "a heaven of mildness". This is a well-worn seduction ploy.

At the same time as Satan professes to worship and look up to Eve, he begins to patronise her, like a courtier with a country maid. Her beauty deserves to be "universally admired", but she has only beasts to appreciate her, which are "beholders rude" (lacking sophistication); and, of course, only one man. "And what is one?" asks Satan, claiming Eve

...shouldst be seen
A goddess among gods, adored and served
By angels numberless, thy daily train...
[IX. 546-8]

Satan is still cleverly keeping his terms vague, allowing ideas to creep into Eve's mind disguised as metaphors. Thus, "gods" can mean only 'angels' (and often does in *Paradise Lost*), so that to be "seen a goddess" might only mean to be regarded as *like* an angel, which is not too alarmingly blasphemous. By the next line, however, she is definitely a deity, and is now being adored by real angels – a dizzying progression.

Eve is no fool, and she does question the serpent – though, fatally, she concentrates upon how the serpent can speak to her, rather than why he does. Her guilelessness allows Satan to attribute magic properties to the fruit – or, rather, to some unnamed fruit, for Satan cunningly does not reveal that he is referring to the forbidden tree until he has lured Eve to its very foot. Her reaction when she sees where she has been led is entirely right. She may have been flattered; she may have *almost* flirted with the serpent (the modesty of lines 615-6 is dangerously close to a mock-modesty which is greedy for more praise); but she is "yet sinless". [IX. 659]

Satan summons up all his powers of rhetoric for the final assault:

...now more bold
The tempter, but with show of zeal and love
To man, and indignation at his wrong,
New part puts on, and as to passion moved,
Fluctuates disturbed, yet comely and in act
Raised, as of some great matter to begin.
As when of old some orator renowned

In Athens or free Rome, where eloquence
Flourished, since mute, to some great cause
addressed,
Stood in himself collected, while each part,
Motion, each act won audience ere the tongue,
Sometimes in highth begun, as no delay
Of preface brooking through his zeal of right.
So standing, moving, or to highth upgrown
The temper all impassioned thus began.
[IX. 664-678]

This is sincerely impassioned hypocrisy. Like all great actors Satan truly becomes his part. Instead of feelings expressing themselves in actions, acting creates disconcertingly real feelings, like the Player King in *Hamlet*, who summons up disturbingly real tears in a fake situation.

Milton's syntax suggests a similar kind of false emotion. Satan starts with acting, "as to passion moved", yet in the next line "fluctuates disturbed". If Satan is so well able to deceive because of his capacity for self-deception, he is nevertheless able to command an audience by his self-control. Like Beelzebub, he can compel attention even before he speaks: "each act won audience ere the tongue". He is described as an orator with complete mastery over himself: he "stood in himself collected".

HEAVENLY RHETORIC

Satan abuses rhetoric: but then Satan always "perverts best things". Milton does not make the facile assumption that because Satan's word-spinning is counter-logically seductive, 'true' oratory is therefore governed by logic.

Adam and Eve in Paradise speak great poetry. To take just one example: Eve invents the first love song of Eden, [IV. 639-56] and it is linguistically highly patterned: the elaborate circling (rhetorical epanalepsis) specifically imitates the suspension of time in the intensity of love, since "With thee conversing I forget all time..."

Great poetry is, as Milton wrote, "subsequent or indeed rather precedent" to both logic and rhetoric. And, like love, innocence or happiness, great poetry is mysterious. It cannot be willed into being.

Milton's description of his own creative processes in *Paradise Lost* represents them as startlingly, thrillingly, even dangerously counter-logical. He uses images of soaring flight that counterpoise those devilish images of hovering and self-raising. The shadows of possible presumption and error are there even in Milton's most sublimely confident assertions that he is divinely inspired. He knows how easy it is for poetry attempting to soar "above the height of Pegasean wing" to become "a flying steed unrefined". [VII. 4, 17]

Milton's "song" is "adventurous", "that with no middle flight intends to soar / Above the Aonian mount" [I. 13-5], even though Satan is the "great adventurer" [X. 440], and "adventurous Eve" [IX. 921] is altogether too "bold".

Poetry is illumination from the darkest places in the human mind. It is both willed yet deeply unwillable; both passive and active.

Milton shows that his poetry comes as much from the dark as the light. It is born of night, the darkness of blindness and the subconscious, in which God "dictates to me slumbering". [IX. 23] The paradoxes of light dwelling in darkness begin in the autobiographical section in the introduction to Book III, where Milton describes and laments his blindness, where his eyes "roll in vain" and "find no dawn". In the night, however, he recites poetry to himself, and especially Hebrew poetry. [III. 30]

But secret processes are taking place as he repeats the poetry:

> *Then feed on thoughts, that voluntary move*
> *Harmonious numbers; as the wakeful bird*
> *Sings darkling, and in shadiest covert hid*
> *Tunes her nocturnal note.*
>
> *[III. 37-40]*

Repeating poetry is a "voluntary" act, as creating it is not: his thoughts "move" the rhythmic measures of the verse; and he is like a "wakeful" and therefore conscious nightingale singing in the dark. But the nightingale is learning as well as singing: she "in shadiest covert hid / Tunes her nocturnal note". It is a darkling description of how Milton by reciting poetry was at the same time subconsciously, covertly learning his art. He turns to his own Muse only at line 51. The muses of others are introduced by negative indirections ("Yet not the more... nor sometimes forget..."); his own by a double positive, "So much the rather..." It is an inner blaze of light in the external darkness of blindness. Yet the description six books later of the *modus operandi* of his inspiration has disconcerted many readers by its emphasis upon how far it lies outside his conscious control. His Muse is a

> *...celestial patroness, who deigns*
> *Her nightly visitations unimplored,*
> *And dictates to me slumbering, or inspires*
> *Easy my unpremeditated verse...*
>
> *[IX. 21-5]*

This may not be quite as extreme as it sounds. Milton may not be intending to suggest that every word of *Paradise Lost* was recited to him. "Dictate" may only mean "command". (When God inspired the prophets and evangelists who wrote the Bible, it was often claimed that his earthly "secretaries" were left to find the words by which to express divinely-inspired concepts. God gave the ideas, but not the form.) Yet Milton goes out of his way to suggest that his poetry has moved far beyond conscious effort. His verse is "easy", and "unpremeditated". Long years of premeditation are certainly there, but are now firmly in the past: "...this subject for heroic song / Pleased me long choosing, and beginning late". [IX. 26-7] The long delay is over; and after all those "sedulous" years his poetry now comes from places beyond planning.◆

What finally makes Eve choose wrong?

The final assault on Eve's virtue is a flurry of half-formed metaphysical and theological arguments. As Barbara Lewalski puts it:

> He confronts Eve with a barrage of definition, false syllogisms and rhetorical questions, subtly complimenting those rational powers wherein she knows herself inferior to Adam. His strategy is to force her to think very quickly about a host of difficult questions and his answers to them, to reel before the shifting meaning he ascribes to such terms as God, the gods, death, knowledge, good and evil. By such means he leads her to analyse the prohibition she once knew to be outside the province of reason, as if it were some obscure oracle requiring elaborate critical interpretation.

Look closely, and one can spot the shifts: Satan suggests that Eve will not die [685], then that she will, but only in order to become a god; he says that because she "fears... death" she should not and cannot fear God; but also that she should *not* fear death, "death to be wished". [714] He suggests both that God forbids the fruit from envy, and that envy cannot dwell in "heavenly breasts". He shifts "virtue", as usual, towards its pagan interpretation of mere courage, suggesting that God will actually praise her "dauntless virtue" in taking the apple, as though the divine prohibition was a merely a 'dare'.

The most important equivocations of all are his attempts to confuse the meanings of "know" and "knowledge". Knowledge can be either 'theoretical' or 'experimental'; and it is possible to understand or know something without knowing it by experience. One does not have to commit parricide, in a necessarily one-off experiment, to learn that killing one's father is wrong. The knowledge of good and evil offered by the fruit of the forbidden tree is, most biblical commentators agree, only experimental. Adam and Eve are fully instructed in and fully cognisant of the nature of good and evil: they gain no theoretical knowledge from the fall, but only the bitter personal experience of loss. After the Fall, when Adam laments that his eyes were indeed opened to "know / Both good and evil", he complains that this is not a true increase in wisdom. His experimental knowledge is actually *less* than his theoretical, since he can feelingly perceive only "good lost, and evil got". [IX. 1072]

Satan, however, insists that God cannot mean that Eve should be "deterred"

from achieving what might lead
To happier life, knowledge of good and evil;
Of good, how just? Of evil, if what is evil

Be real, why not known, since easier shunned?
[IX. 696-699]

This is cleverly compressed to near-incomprehensibility; but Satan manages to suggest that the only true knowledge is an experimental knowledge gained by plucking the fruit, and thus only by embracing evil can evil be "shunned".

None of Satan's arguments are quite coherent; and, cunningly, he does not rest his case on any single one of them:

These, and many more
Causes import your need of this fair fruit.
[IX. 370-1]

Pure slick advertising: the fruit is now a "must-have item," which is how modern tempters describe something entirely unnecessary and hideously over-priced. Indeed, what Satan is saying to Eve throughout his temptation is "because you're *worth* it".

That verb "import" punningly suggests to us that her "need" is not innate, but introduced into her. And significantly Eve, in her response to Satan, merely repeats Satan's arguments and phrases without adding anything of her own. "Pausing awhile, thus to herself she mused", but without addressing herself convincingly to any one argument. As William Empson perceptively remarked in reply to the question of exactly why Eve fell:

> I think that Milton would have said that Eve did not know why, any more than all we critics do; a lot of arguments have come before her, and she would not know which of them made her decide.

Satan has tempted her into "speculations high or deep" [IX. 602]; and she is trying to emulate a God-like ability to hold all things in her mind at once. Too many causes blur until she engages with none of them – a slipping of the gears of conscience. Eve's last words before she picks the fruit are the equivalent only of "why not?"

> *What hinders then*
> *To reach, and feed at once both body and mind?*
> *[IX. 778-9]*

Milton manages to suggest a sort of causeless cause: he makes us feel how an act of wrongdoing can come to seem so *easy*. "What hinders then..." and her hand, "in evil hour/ Forth reaching to the fruit", performs the deed, seemingly almost by itself.

How does Milton portray the fall of Adam?

Interestingly, Milton's poetic imagination is more engaged with Eve than it is with Adam: we are shown her in her daily life, gardening, gathering fruits for lunch; she is given two great temptation scenes; and she is the tragic heroine (or anti-heroine) of the poem. She is even given, quite literally, the last word in *Paradise Lost.* In epic poetry, the last directly reported speech is usually reserved for the hero; and Eve's final 14 lines – an unrhymed sonnet of farewell, balancing loss and hope – bring us back to her at the end of the poem.

Milton goes far beyond the demands of Christian orthodoxy in imagining Eve as an individual. He never takes the easy misogynist shortcuts of the period, never representing her, for example, as the "weaker vessel", prey to the lower lusts of the flesh, and therefore by nature a temptress. Milton explores in Eve frailties not of the flesh but of the intellect, and particularly of the overburdened mind under the pressures of solitude and delay – pressures which Milton, the blind scholar waiting in political exile, himself knew intimately.

If Milton is interested in Eve as an individual, he is chiefly interested in Adam through his relationship with Eve. Eve's fall comes first; and Adam only falls because she does.

Adam's fall is made almost the mirror-image of Eve's. If we – and she – hardly know why Eve falls, we – and he – know exactly why Adam does. He falls "for vehemence of love". The question is to what extent we should censure this.

If Eve has two temptations by Satan himself, Adam has none. Eve, when Satan insinuates himself into her mind, has instinctively the right reactions: she recoils in horror. If she had not been lured into thinking, into that fatal delay, into "looking into the air too long", she would not have fallen.

Adam's fall is the opposite of this. His immediate and instinctive reaction is the wrong one. If he had delayed, or allowed himself to think things through, he would not have fallen at all.

Adam's fall takes place not only without delay, before thought, but seemingly almost before conscious reaction. There are intimations of this even before he knows what has taken place. Waiting for Eve's return from her dangerously solitary labours, he weaves a garland to crown her,

Yet oft his heart, divine of something ill,
Misgave him; he the faltering measure felt...

[IX. 845-6]

A wonderfully faltering rhythm conveys the inwardness of this misgiving, and his heart does misgive him, in the sense of giving him away. When Adam discovers that Eve has disobeyed God, he is stunned and bewildered – "astonied", as Milton puts it. "Astonied" is more powerful than our modern "astonished": it comes from the Latin 'to strike with a thunderbolt'. In that moment of dazed nullity – a white-sheet blankness – his non-decision seems made:

On the other side, Adam, soon as he heard
The fatal trespass done by Eve, amazed,
Astonied stood and blank, while horror chill
Ran through his veins, and all his joints relaxed;
From his slack hand the garland wreathed for Eve
Down dropped, and all the faded roses shed:
Speechless he stood and pale, till thus at length
First to himself he inward silence broke.
[IX. 888-95]

Eve's "venturesome arm", her "rash hand", reaching out as if by itself, has its counter-image in Adam's "slack hand", letting go the garland. Eve seems to watch herself doing it; Adam does not see it happening at all. The garland falling from his slack hand is a detail cinematic in its immediacy, loaded with significance. The roses are fading: the first sign of mutability in Paradise. The roses that showered petals upon Adam and Eve's nuptial bed "repaired" themselves by next morning, just as their love was perpetually renewed: now, earthly bliss is irrevocably falling apart.

Adam's pause is one of blankness, not

hesitation. When he speaks, he has already made up his mind: "Certain my resolution is to die..."

There is proper tragic ambiguity in both Falls. Is Adam more or less to blame than Eve? Those who sin knowingly are surely more to blame; yet how much do we blame Adam, who, though "not deceived", nevertheless knowingly decided to die because he loved his wife so much?

If *Paradise Lost* is a great poem, it is because Milton does not short-circuit these ambiguities. When he sums up Adam as one who was "not deceived... but fondly overcome by female charm"[IX. 998-9], it is shocking: this is not the noble Adam we have seen, who composed love poetry to the woman he adored. But this summing-up is meant to be shocking: it is a measure of how far he has fallen that this is what Adam has now become. The tragedy of *Paradise Lost* lies in just this sense of loss, of infinite potential ruined. We are all woefully defined by our wrong choices. Just as Satan, the "arch-angel ruined", redefines himself into a mere serpent, Adam becomes a doting fool.

Is Eve inferior to Adam?

Adam falls from "vehemence of love"; but in what way are we supposed to condemn him for this? Is his sin mere lust, or loving too much? And is his "slack hand" meant to suggest an inability to exercise proper control over his wife?

To answer this, it is important to understand how and in what way Milton believed – as he did – that men should rule over women.

Milton's 'patriarchy' is never simplistic or misogynist. Indeed some critics, such as Philip Gallagher, see Milton as a 'proto-feminist'. Gallagher points out that whenever there are gaps in the Biblical story to be filled, Milton shifts his interpretation of Genesis away from conventional misogyny to give Eve more sympathy, and more equality. For example, the Bible gives Adam alone

EVE'S RINGLETS

Feminists often object to Milton introducing Eve with "dishevelled" hair, curling in "wanton ringlets" [IV. 305], thus, they say, casting her as a temptress by nature. But there is no bias against Eve in this description. The wanton ringlets are, as Fowler observes, "as poignantly innocent as Paradise's mazy 'errors'", though an image suggesting fragility and a hint of the Fall to come; and there is exactly the same ambiguity in the description of Adam's hair, whose tightly clustering curls are called "hyacinthine". [IV. 301]

This is an heroic Homeric epithet; yet the classical myth of the beautiful youth Hyacinthus was understood as an emblem of weakness, showing, according to George Sandys, that "the natural understanding, when innocent and uncorrupted, resembles a boy; that is, wanting wisdom". ◆

the task of naming all created beings: his bestowal of true names is a sign not only of his dominion over the creature kingdom, but also of his instinctive wisdom.

Milton, however, not only makes Eve share in Adam's "naked majesty" [IV. 290] and "dominion given / Over all other creatures" (IV. 430-1), but also, rather remarkably, says that she has named the plants in Paradise. [XI. 277] She is, in every way, "accomplished Eve". [IV. 660] When Adam and Raphael have their discussion about astronomy, and Eve leaves to tend her plants, Milton goes out of his way to insist that this is not because she is unable to understand such abstruse matters:

> *Yet went she not, as not with such discourse*
> *Delighted, or not capable her ear*
> *Of what was high...*
>
> *[VIII. 48-50]*

But if Milton is sympathetic to Eve, it is going too far to call him"the first great feminist in Western culture".

In truth, Milton is no more a feminist than he is a misogynist. He is a man of his age; and the ambiguities in his view of the relationship between the sexes stem from the Bible and, in particular, the letters attributed to St Paul. These contain both the most liberating statements of absolute equality between the sexes, and the most authoritarian assertions of male supremacy. The revolutionary core of the Bible is summed up by St Paul in Galatians 3.26-8:

> ye are all the children of God by faith in Christ Jesus... There is neither Jew nor Greek, there is neither bond nor free, there is neither male nor female: for ye are all one in Christ Jesus.

But in Timothy 2.11-13 there is a different message:

> Let the woman learn in silence with all subjection. But suffer not a woman to teach, nor to usurp authority over the man, but to be in silence. For Adam was first formed, then Eve.

That Milton was a man of his age does not that he mean that he was therefore 'trapped' by his Christianity into a particular view of women. The ambiguities in the Bible offer – for a Protestant, even demand – a personal interpretation.

Milton's own position was however perhaps *less* radical than modern readers might expect, given his obsession with liberty. He never equated liberty with equality; and while many Puritans believed that all human beings were equal, since all were equally worthless on their own merits, Milton strongly believed that some men were worthier than others – and that most men were, as a general rule, worthier than most women*. If "reason also is choice", men possess "the higher intellectual" (see opposite).

In *Paradise Lost*, when Adam and Eve are first introduced, in "naked majesty", they show both equality and hierarchy:

Two of far nobler shape erect and tall
Godlike erect, with native honour clad
In naked majesty seemed lords of all,
And worthy seemed, for in their looks divine
The image of their glorious maker shone,
Truth, wisdom, sanctitude severe and pure,
Severe but in true filial freedom placed;
Whence true authority in men; though both
Not equal, as their sex not equal seemed;
For contemplation he and valour formed,
For softness she and sweet attractive grace,
He for God only, she for God in him.

[IV. 288-99]

They are both made in the image of their maker. Both have majesty and "filial freedom", so that they are siblings in God, and D.M. Friedman may be right to argue that here "not equal"

*In his divorce pamphlets, Milton did notice that, in this fallen world, women could be wiser and better than men. In that case, he decided, the woman should rule in the marriage. It is a sort of sexual republicanism – one that may be necessary in the fallen world, but not in Paradise.

means "not the same".

In his later conversation with Raphael, however, Adam says – and is not corrected by the angel – that Eve is a less perfect image of God.

She is:

> *...in outward show*
> *Elaborate, of inward less exact.*
> *For well I understand in the prime end*
> *Of nature her the inferior, in the mind*
> *And inward faculties, which most excel,*
> *In outward also her resembling less*
> *His image who made both...*
>
> *[VII. 538-544]*

WHAT IS ADAM'S "HIGHER INTELLECTUAL"?

Adam, according to Satan, possesses a " higher intellectual" than Eve. [XI. 483] But Milton is not here affirming that men are cleverer than women, or even that they are more rational. In Milton's world, the distinction between the 'higher' and the 'lower' forms of reason was more like the difference between pure and applied mathematics.

Augustine divided the human intellect or reason into ratio superior/ sublimior and ratio inferior. 'Lower' reason was directed towards the created world. It involved the memorizing, rational analysis and comprehension of all data

This is Adam before the Fall. Afterwards, he becomes aggressively misogynist in his recriminations, describing Eve as but a "rib / Crooked by nature", a "fair defect / Of nature" (Aristotle defined woman as a defective man) , a temptress whose meretricious sexuality "snares" men. These are stock gibes against women, clichés of that age; but Milton evidently intends them to be shocking: a mark of just how far Adam has fallen from the exalted tenderness and reverence with which he once adored his wife. Apart from the obvious unfair nastiness, Adam is clearly wrong because he is accusing nature of being defective, which is to accuse God of having mis-made her.

gathered by the senses: its end was scientia – i.e. 'knowledge'. Empirical science would however certainly fall within the remit of Eve's 'lower reason'.

'Higher' reason was directed towards eternal verities, judging corporeal things by incorporeal and unchangeable truths. Its true end was not scientia but sapientia – not knowledge, but wisdom. 'Lower' reason was directed towards action, the 'higher', towards contemplation. Milton's describes the right way to heaven, through "contemplation of created things" [V. 511], as a fusion of higher and lower reason.

On the metaphorical level, Adam and Eve should be viewed as different aspects of a single human psyche: *Paradise Lost* is an exploration of a single act of choice.

But even on the literal level, the relationship between Adam and Eve is a world apart even from our modern stereotypes. There is no division into egghead and airhead.◆

He comes dangerously close to doing this in his earlier, pre-Fall conversation with Raphael. Significantly, though, unfallen Adam is much more worried about possible deficiencies in *himself*. He feels too susceptible to Eve's charms:

> *...Or nature failed in me, and left some part*
> *Not proof enough such object to sustain...*
> *[VIII. 534-5]*

Raphael does not correct Adam when he says Eve is inferior to him, but he does pull him up short when he wonders if nature has failed: "Accuse not nature". [VIII. 561]

If Eve is inferior, it is certainly not because she is in any way defective, and Adam's reverent prelapsarian love of Eve is not, in Milton's Paradise, incompatible with hierarchy. In Paradise, all hierarchy is consensual, and all obedience willing. It is not in the nature of unfallen Adam to command Eve to do anything that does not bring her delight. God himself, Milton argues in *De Doctrina Christiana,* is bound by his own laws: he cannot be capricious, cruel or tyrannical in his commands. Despite his omnipotence, therefore, even God cannot force anyone to do his will, since all forcing of obedience is 'tyranny' and all enforced obedience 'slavery'. In these circumstances, *true* hierarchy cannot ever be irksome.

Is sex in Paradise innocent or dangerous?

Sex, the fourth of Solomon's "wonderful things" – "the way of a man with a maid" – is never far from Paradise. It is there in Satan's seduction of Eve, with Cavalier love-poetry. One does not have to rely on Freudian interpretations of an upright serpent to see this as sexual: the innocent pastoral maiden is left "deflowered" [X. 901] by a sophisticated intruder.*

The counter-logical lure of sex is vital in *Paradise Lost*; it is not, however, evil. Milton's attitude towards sex was shaped by his unorthodox views on the relationship between spirit and matter, or soul and body.

In his early poems, Milton seems to have been a conventional Neo-platonic Christian, describing the soul as a pure spirit trapped in a "darksome house of mortal clay". By the time he wrote *Paradise Lost*, however, he had rejected the idea that there is a dichotomy – or division – between matter and spirit. He became, in effect, a highly individual "monist" (see opposite).

His change of mind emerges in his theological treatise, *De Doctrina Christiana*, where he puts

* Even the *landscape* in Paradise is sexualized, as C.S. Lewis noted. The schoolboy who finds innuendo in the "swelling gourd" and "bush with frizzled hair implicit" [VII. 321-3] may be wiser in his generation than his disapproving schoolmaster.

forward the extremely unorthodox notion that all of material creation was not made *ex nihilo*, out of nothing, but *ex deo*, out of God. What he calls, in *Paradise Lost*, the "dark materials" of the human body [II. 916] are derived by God from himself. All matter is therefore good; and the difference between matter and spirit is not one of substance but degree. Body and soul are on a continuum, a sort of sliding scale, varying only in the degree to which this substance derived from God is "airy" or "refined". As Raphael expounds to Adam:

O Adam, one Almighty is, from whom

MILTON, DONNE AND MONISM

Milton truly believed in the notion that Donne only played with – a continuum between mind and body, i.e. monism. Donne wrote, in an elegy for a girl he had never met, that "one might almost say, her body thought"; and T.S.Eliot seized on this to spin the thesis that Donne – unlike Milton – possessed a peculiarly unified sensibility, in which sensation is united with thought. "A thought to Donne was an experience: it modified his sensibility." With Milton, according to Eliot, a "dissociation of sensibility" sets in.

Even without this theory, most readers would probably categorize Donne as a love-poet, and Milton as an austere Puritan. Yet, arguably, Eliot got his thesis completely back to front. Donne, one might claim, is exhilarating and startling precisely because he possesses perhaps the most brilliantly disconcerting,

All things proceed, and up to him return,
If not depraved from good, created all
Such to perfection, one first matter all,
Indued with various forms, various degrees
Of substance, and in things that live, of life;
But more refined, more spirituous, and pure,
As nearer to him placed or nearer tending
Each in their several active spheres assigned,
Till body up to spirit work, in bounds
Proportioned to each kind. So from the root
Springs lighter the green stalk, from thence the leaves

---

restless and self-consciously "dissociated" sensibility ever to write great poetry. There is nothing unifying about his poems, in which thoughts destroy feelings, feelings undermine thoughts; and poetry itself can alter both.

It is Milton, not Donne, who glorifies human love. Donne's sermons regard sex even in marriage with suspicion; Milton celebrates sex as its crowning glory. Nor can one write off Donne's preachings as a simple case of youthful libertinism hardening into reactionary old age. Donne's greatest youthful love-lyrics often seem to be hardly love-poems at all. Milton's Adam knows longing, and even physical desire, in a way that Donne's protagonists do not: Adam, who reveres the sheer otherness of the woman he loves, is utterly unlike Donne. Donne's poems know that the poet can argue a woman into bed, or himself out of love, with terrifyingly equal facility.

Christopher Ricks, indeed, suggests that Donne's lyrics regularly end in "post-coital sadness and

More airy, last the bright consummate flower
Spirits odorous breathes...

[V. 469-482]

The created universe is then like a single organism, of which Adam and Eve are only part, and plant-nurturing Eve is like the first eco-heroine. Men and angels are both part of the same scale, "differing but in degree, of kind the same". The strand of thinking that ties together "the world, the flesh and the devil" is dissolved.

Flesh is good: Milton is the poet who had to

revulsion". Certainly, they characteristically undermine themselves: 'A Lecture upon the Shadow', for example, which conjures up a brief, "brave clearness" in love, ends with the notion that "Love is a growing, or full constant light, / And his first minute, after noon, is night." This is about as celebratory, or reassuring, as Woody Allen's neurotic simile: "A relationship, I think, is like a shark. You know? It has to move constantly forward or it dies. And I think what we got on our hands is a dead shark."

T.S.Eliot claimed Donne could "devour any kind of experience", but this is equally if not more true of Milton. It is Milton, however, whose encyclopaedic poetry attempts – with a quite extraordinary degree of success – to "unify" elements of "disparate experience".

This is not, of course, to claim that Milton is a greater poet than Donne, but only to suggest that the differences between them are not what modern readers regularly assume.◆

coin a new word, "sensuous", to express a radical idea of innocent sensuality. And *Paradise Lost* is full of innocent concupiscence. It was Milton's deliberate and unusual choice to give Adam and Eve a happy and fulfilled prelapsarian sex life: the majority of commentators believed that they fell on the day of their creation, and that sex came post-Fall, so that murderous Cain and his twin brother Abel were conceived in sin.

In *Paradise Lost* not only humans but angels have sex. The angels' bodies of compacted air are on the "spirituous" end of the scale: their "essence pure" is "soft / And uncompounded". [I. 424-5] Rather disconcertingly, this means that they "can either sex assume / Or both" (a feat which in the natural world is emulated by the humble slug: apparently all slugs north of Manchester mate only with themselves). Adam questions Raphael on the details, and is told that it involves total interpenetration:

Whatever pure thou in the body enjoyst
(And pure thou wert created) we enjoy
In eminence, and obstacle find none
Of membrane, joint, or limb, exclusive bars:
Easier than air with air, if spirits embrace,
Total they mix, union of pure with pure
Desiring; nor restrained conveyance need
As flesh to mix with flesh, or soul with soul.
[VIII. 622-9]

Only angels, it seems, can go all the way.

Whether the fallen angels enjoy sex is less clear, though the fallen angels in the Bible slept with the "daughters of men". Empson pointed out that in *Paradise Lost* the devils are associated with sterility ("frozen loins", [I. 352]), and with the torments of unfulfilled desire. Satan in Paradise is a leering voyeur, watching Adam and Eve kiss, and jealous of the pleasure he cannot share. [IV. 501-11]

Satan's daughter, Sin, is conceived in perverted solitude, his allegorical brain-child. The conception is distinctly like a sexual spasm, but one involving pain, rather than pleasure – somewhere between masturbation and a caesarean without anaesthetic:

> *All on a sudden miserable pain*
> *Surprised thee, dim thine eyes, and dizzy swum*
> *In darkness...*
>
> *[II. 753-5]*

Dizziness and dimming of eyesight during orgasm were cited by Tertullian as evidence that part of the soul was passing out of the body during ejaculation: a 'little death', which was thought to shorten one's lifespan. Satanic sex leads to death, not life, even before it moves on to incest and incestuous rape.

How much do Adam and Eve need each other?

Adam and Eve need each other: "It is not good for man to be alone". But their awareness of their need for each other, which is part of their love, is subtly differentiated. Eve is not always aware of how much and in what way she needs Adam: her illusions of independence are dangerous. In contrast, Adam is fully aware of how much he needs Eve. This is wise; but risky. Awareness of need may become neediness.

Describing someone as 'needy' is very modern, but Milton would have understood it (see below). In *Paradise Lost,* Milton explores the psychology of the need of others, and its relationship to a

MILTON'S MARRIAGE

Milton's descriptions in his pamphlets of how marriage based on need can founder in such circumstances are so vehement, and so specific, that it is impossible not to read them as being based on his own "lamented experience".

His own disastrous first marriage seems to have been precipitated by the pressures of 'unkind solitariness', or unnatural loneliness. In his pamphlets on divorce, Milton described how the longing for companionship is a "rational burning" that runs deeper and is harder to quell than merely lustful longings.
Milton married in haste in 1642, bringing home his first wife, Mary Powell after a

fragile and contingent sense of self. Both Adam and Eve are given vivid descriptions of their earliest memories, including their developing sense of self-hood. Eve's account comes first, told to Adam. The delay before she sets eyes on Adam is entirely Milton's invention. Like all delay in Milton, it is a space for psychological exploration:

That day I oft remember, when from sleep
I first awakened, and found myself reposed
Under a shade on flowers, much wondering where
And what I was, whence thither brought, and how.
Not distant far from thence a murmuring sound
Of waters issued from a cave and spread
Into a liquid plain, then stood unmoved
Pure as the expanse of heaven; I thither went

month's stay in the country. He was 34, and she was 17. He had failed entirely to recognise the signs of incompatibility; and found himself "yoked" to a "mute and spiritless mate". Sex without love he found to be a form of slavery: a grinding "in the mill of an undelighted and servile copulation".

Mary Powell left Milton shortly after the marriage, returning to her mother; in her absence, Milton wrote his pamphlets urging that divorce should be permitted on grounds of incompatibility – a notion, as Barbara Lewalski points out, "virtually unheard of in England". After three years,Mary was reconciled to her husband; and the marriage in fact lasted until 1652, when Mary died in childbirth. Milton married twice more. His second wife, Katherine Woodcock, also died after giving birth. His third wife, Elizabeth Minshull, survived him. ◆

With unexperienced thought, and laid me down
On the green bank to look into the clear
Smooth lake, that to me seemed another sky.
As I bent down to look, just opposite,
A shape within the watery gleam appeared
Bending to look on me, I started back,
It started back, but pleased I soon returned,
Pleased it returned as soon with answering looks
Of sympathy and love; there had I fixed
Mine eyes till now, and pined with vain desire,
Had not a voice thus warned me, What thou seest,
What there thou seest fair creature is thyself...
[IV. 449-68]

Eve, like Narcissus, seems to fall in love with herself, and pines with "vain desire". This could suggest that women are prone to mirror-gazing, vanity and self-love, and need to learn to be ruled by the higher wisdom of men.

But while this superficial 'moral' may be there, Milton is actually concerned with something more universal: our need to become aware of others before we can be truly aware of ourselves. Eve is represented on the borders of self-consciousness. Her thoughts are "unexperienced". She lacks experience; she may not even be conscious of what she is thinking. In this dream-like state of acute awareness without consciousness of self, she looks into the "unmoved lake", which offers the calm of both literal and metaphorical reflection. Becoming enraptured by her reflection is not so much an image of self-love as of a lack of self-knowledge: she literally does not know herself.

It is impossible to blame her for this, since she has as yet known nothing else. But when the "voice" directs her towards Adam, she has a choice: between illusion – her own fair "shadow" – and true substance – the real man who gave her "substantial life". [IV. 485] She hesitates: Adam seems "less winning soft, less amiably mild" than her "smooth watry image"; but Adam tenderly woos her, and "gently" seizes her hand. It is a moment in which Adam's hand acts rightly, gentle but decisive.

Eve, by yielding to him, makes her choice, and it is for moral substance over the "shadow" of physical beauty: "wisdom, which alone is truly fair". There is a clear moral hierarchy here; yet Eve's movement towards true love is not conventionally Neoplatonic. That would involve starting with carnal love, then recognising fleshly things to be only a shadow, discarding them and moving up the ladder to a higher, spiritual level. But Eve's love of her "watry shadow" is hardly fleshly. She is represented more as a half-awakened girl still in love with her own imaginings, who needs to be gently drawn into realising that "substantial" love of a real – and fleshly – man is better than "vain desire" for something that does not exist.

When Eve does fall in love with Adam, it is not his body that initially attracts her: she does not find it "winning". Eve is won by his eloquence and by his need for her. From this, she falls in love with his mind. Attributing superior wisdom to those who fall in love with you is natural, though only safe in Paradise. Of course, there are possible moral dangers here. Though Eve playing with her reflection is innocent, there is an echo of how Satan is drawn to his daughter Sin: "Thyself in me thy perfect image/ Becamst enamoured". [II. 764-5] And Eve's susceptibility to being wooed, her tendency to be overawed by imagined as well as real superior wisdom, and to be dazzled by rhetoric, will all contribute to her fall.

Adam's description of his awakening, related to Raphael, makes a companion-piece to Eve's – alike yet offering deliberate contrasts. He too awakes "from soundest sleep", with no knowledge of "who I was, or where, or from what cause". [VIII. 253ff] Instinctively, as befits the "higher intellectual", he looks up, "straight toward heaven my wandering eyes I turned"; but Nature alone cannot reveal the existence of God.

Divine intervention is needed to take him beyond the state of a noble savage, who can only "feel that I am happier than I know". In a dream, a divine guide floats him to Paradise, "as in air / Smooth sliding without step". This is a 'good' version of Eve's 'flying' dream: he is taken "by the hand”, safely “led”, placed in an orchard of “tempting” but unforbidden fruits, and wakes to find the dream not delusive, but true.

Adam’s self-knowledge grows by stages. He understands the true natures of the animals as he names them; but learns from them the nature of his own solitude. He begins to understand what to ask for, and pleads above all for “fellowship”. “True delight” can only be found in a “mutual” relationship between equals.

Adam realises and declares with proper humility that, if he needs a companion, it is because he is not like God, who is perfect in and of himself. Man can only aspire to perfection; and he argues that “the cause of his desire” is the need for mutual help in this upward climb, “by conversation with his like to help / Or solace his defects”. [VIII. 418-9] Society itself is bound together for mutual help, in “collateral love and dearest amity”. A solitary man, Adam says, is “single imperfection”, “unity defective”. [VIII. 423-6]

Adam’s awareness of what he lacks helps to cause the Fall, since his need for companionship leads to the creation of Eve. Yet his awareness of his need for Eve is explicitly approved by God. It is, God says, a sign of wisdom, knowledge “not of beasts alone... but of thyself”. It will be Adam’s tragedy that this wisdom is warped into weakness.

How innocent is Adam's passion for Eve?

Adam asks for fellowship; what he gets, beyond his asking or imagining, is love. Under God's forming hands "a creature grew", whose looks "from that time infused / Sweetness into my heart unfelt before". [VIII. 474-5] Eve hesitates before choosing Adam. For Adam there is no hesitation – no choice, even. Eve is, after all, tailor-made for him, "thy wish, exactly to thy heart's desire".

But this is the 'no choice' feeling of absolute love, not the 'no choice' feeling of 'no one else available'. When Eve has fallen, Adam recognises that there could be a choice: God could make him a second Eve. But it is *this* one he loves, and that seems beyond choice:

> *Should God create another Eve, and I*
> *Another rib afford, yet loss of thee*
> *Would never from my heart...*
>
> *[IX. 911-3]*

Falling completely and irrevocably in love at first sight is not wrong, of course, yet it is extraordinary how passionate, unwilled, counter-logical and sexually charged Milton makes Adam's prelapsarian feelings.

This is not orthodox. Augustine imagined Adam and Eve's unfallen relationship as devoid of all passion and desire, and struggles to imagine them – even potentially – having passion-free sex in order to fulfil the divine command to "go forth and multiply". Augustine offers a singularly unattractive solution: willed coition, with the genitals under complete control, undisturbed by any sexual excitement or gratification, performed solely for the purpose of procreation.

Unlike Augustine, Milton wisely leaves the mechanics attractively vague. The genitals remain "mysterious parts" [IV. 312], though not hidden in shame; and what Milton celebrates in his hymn to "wedded Love" is the deep mysteriousness of sex, which, like the mysteries of religion, lies beyond reason: the "rites / Mysterious of connubial love", obeying a "mysterious law". [IV. 743-50]

Post-Augustine, Christians came to see passionate love as the sign of man's fallen state, but Milton disagrees . He defiantly stresses that love for Eve alters Adam's mind even when he is still innocent. For Adam, sexual desire is not just one among many kinds of 'concupiscence', as it is for Augustine; it is mysteriously and qualitatively different from other pleasures. As Adam tells Raphael, he finds

In all things else delight indeed, but such
As used or not, works in the mind no change,
Nor vehement desire...

[VIII. 524-6]

With Eve,

Far otherwise, transported I behold
Transported touch; here passion first I felt
Commotion strange, in all enjoyments else
Superior and unmoved...

[VIII. 529-32]

Turbulent intensity is in Christian convention the sign of rebellious lusts, not innocent love. Yet would it be better for a man in love to remain "superior and unmoved" – the repellent perfection of those who "moving others, are themselves as stone / Unmoved, cold, and to temptation slow"?

There is obvious danger in the kind of passion Adam feels for Eve, and some commentators therefore see *Paradise Lost* as a relatively simple treatise on temperance. Emotions and desires are like the "wanton growth" in the garden, which, although not in itself evil, is always "tending to wild", and in constant need of moral pruning. [IV. 629-30] Excessive love is dangerous.

Adam is aware of this himself. The physical loveliness of Eve tends to deflect attention to "outward show"; and everything she does or says seem to him so absolutely and utterly right ("wisest, virtuousest, discreetest, best") that

All higher knowledge in her presence falls
Degraded, wisdom in discourse with her

Loses discount'nanced, and like folly shows...
[VIII. 550-3]

But while Adam is conscious of the dangers of loving too much, he does not accept Raphael's Neoplatonic warning against "carnal pleasure", or the view that "in loving thou dost well, in passion not". [VIII. 588]

Remarkably, Adam is allowed to question Raphael's strictures. He suggests, from his own experience, that it is impossible to separate love from passion, and that equating passion with mere lust is a false equivalence. He rates sex – "the genial bed" – more highly than the angel does, regarding it with "mysterious reverence"; but his chief point is that his sexual desire and his delight in Eve's physical beauty – "her outside formed so fair" – are only part of his passion. He delights most in *her*, and everything she does:

Those graceful acts,
Those thousand decencies that daily flow
From all her words and actions...
[VIII. 600-2]

"Decencies" means "beauties", but Adam is insisting that what is comely in Eve is also perfectly respectable. Once again, he is hymning the way in which love makes every act of the loved one seem perfect, and right. This, when loving a good and beautiful wife, is not mere carnality. Moreover, he insists that his passionate feelings do not "subject" him. His judgment and will are "still free" to "approve the best, and follow what I approve". [VIII. 611] And then he comes up with the clinching question: how do angels "express their love"? Raphael, blushing "celestial rosy red, love's proper hue", confesses that angels too have a form of pure and total sex.

Passion and desire are part of the innocent pleasures of Paradise. Yet after the Fall, this innocent enthusiasm for sex is the first impulse to be corrupted. The first sign is quasi-drunkenness, with more images of ominously delusive floating and flying:

As with new wine intoxicated both
They swim in mirth, and fancy that they feel,
Divinity within them breeding wings
Wherewith to scorn the earth: but that false fruit
Far other operation first displayed,
Carnal desire inflaming, he on Eve
Began to cast lascivious eyes, she on him
As wantonly repaid; in lust they burn...

[IX. 1013-5]

Adam and Eve still find pleasure in each other, but it is no longer as a way of expressing their love. Instead, sex becomes like a gourmet menu – simply a way of gratifying the senses. Adam congratulates Eve on being "exact of taste" in picking the fruit:

discrimination is now sensual rather than moral. Sex becomes mere after-dinner entertainment. Adam turns to Eve with the chillingly frivolous invitation:

> *But come, so well refreshed, now let us play*
> *As meet is, after such delicious fare.*
>
> *[IX. 1027]*

Even Adam's seizing of Eve's hand is coarsened: "her hand he seized" – no gentleness, now; though she is "nothing loath".

Merely lustful coition is now, as Augustine views all sex, "the seal, / The solace of their sin". [IX. 1043-4] When the couple awake next morning, with the "unkindly fumes" of moral hangovers, they are suffering from acute post-coital *tristesse.*

How does the relationship between Adam and Eve go wrong?

This question has to be framed as 'how' rather than 'why'. This, in many ways, is easy to understand, at least emotionally: we have all known relationships which have deteriorated for no explicable reason - only "the unaccountable and secret reasons of disaffection between man and wife".

It is important that Adam, like Eve, falls for non-reasons. It is interesting what Milton does *not* do: he does not make Adam fall because he is sexually tempted by Eve. Milton could easily have constructed a scene of specifically sexual temptation between a newly fallen Eve and uncorrupted Adam. She could have been shown as like Dalila swooping down on Samson in *Samson Agonistes*:

But who is this, what thing of sea or land?
Female of sex it seems
That so bedecked, ornate and gay
Comes this way sailing
Like a stately ship
Of Tarsus, bound for th'isles
Of Javan or Gadire
With all her bravery on, and tackle trim
Sails filled, and streamers waving
Courted by all the winds that hold them play...
[SA, 710-19]

Sexual allure could, as here, be like a sinister ship. But Eve does not even flaunt her enticing curls. It is not her presence that undoes Adam, so much as her absence, and the prospect of her loss. Propinquity breeds sexual desire; but distance, absence and delay create a different reaction – a longing which can tilt into despair: "Certain my resolution is to die...”

Milton explores the obscure pull created by distance, absence and delay through the pre-Fall sex-games of Adam and Eve, depicting “subtle and wily refluxes” in their relationship, hinting at the possibility of darker patterns of domination and submission. The pattern is set in the first moment of their meeting, when Eve shrinks from Adam. In Eve’s version, this is merely because she does not recognise his superior attractions. Adam’s version is more disturbingly ambiguous. She turns away because of her

Innocence and virgin modesty,
Her virtue and the conscience of her worth
That would be wooed, and not unsought be won,
Not obvious, not obtrusive, but retired,
The more desirable...

[VIII. 501-4]

Innocence and modesty are there; but so too is a sort of coy self-consciousness and artless artfulness. “Conscience of her worth” is bound to be morally precarious. (Satan is “conscious of highest worth” in Book II.) And “retired” is suggestive of those dark places in the human psyche which are like the dark places in the universe from which God has ‘retired’.

This, however, is Adam’s way of seeing her. The fact that she flees makes her “more desirable” to him; but what is truly fascinating is the opacity of her innocence. Just how conscious is she of the effect she is having?

Eve's semi-self-conscious retiring makes her "more desirable": by a brilliant stroke, Milton makes the apparent self-sufficiency which is so dangerous for Eve the source of endless and ultimately fatal fascination for Adam. He exclaims in rapture over her exquisite self-containment: "So absolute she seems/ And in herself complete". [VIII. 547] The line-ending heightens awareness of the danger – this is mere seeming; yet one can feel the compulsive fascination, for Adam, of the sheer *otherness* of Eve. This is a creature who was once literally part of him, but is now completely apart from him, and most strangely and wonderfully "in herself complete."

Separateness and otherness create their own forms of longing. When Eve is undergoing her dream-temptation, Adam wakes first, to find her "with tresses discomposed and glowing cheek". He watches her in her sleep, in a sort of mini-temptation-scene of his own:

...he on his side
Leaning half-raised, with looks of cordial love
Hung over her enamoured, and beheld
Beauty, which whether waking or asleep
Shot forth peculiar graces...

[V. 11-5]

The peculiarity of watching someone sleeping is the combination of tender physical closeness and separation. The sleeper is simultaneously intensely vulnerable, yet utterly inaccessible. Adam, watching, hangs on the brink of obsession. He is enchanted by her "peculiar graces" – the charms that seem to him to be entirely her own. And nothing is stranger than the graces that are peculiar to sleep – when one is least (or most secretly) oneself. These are not the graces of a "fit conversing soul", or of the love that "hath his seat/ In reason".

If separation breeds fascination, delay fires longing. There is delay in the very word "dalliance", whose root lies in "dallying". Playful delay is part of the age-old repertoire of lovers through the ages, even in Milton's Paradise. Love should be, as Milton describes music, "linked sweetness, long drawn out". (Allegro 140) Adam and Eve play games of "sweet reluctant amorous delay". [IV. 311] The delay is "sweet" only because it is entirely gentle and the struggle playfully consensual. The important debate between Adam and Eve over whether Eve should absent herself to work on her own is part of a pattern of flirtatious withdrawal and mastery: a tabloid newspaper would sum up this aspect of the Fall as "The Sex-Game That Went Tragically Wrong".

The debate between Adam and Eve is the nearest they have to a quarrel before the Fall.

Adam and Eve both, of course, choose wrongly at the end of it: Eve in asserting her self-sufficiency, Adam in yielding to it. Critics are divided in apportioning blame: some concentrate on Eve's wilfulness, and love of her own power; some blame Adam for yielding, when he saw the dangers so clearly. Such a division is a clear indication of the superbly balanced moral ambiguities running through the scene.

The arguments of both protagonists are good; but both are based on emotional misunderstandings. The flaw that threatens their relationship is "diffidence", or distrust. In Adam, this comes close to the modern meaning of self-distrust: he first weakens when he imagines (wrongly) that Eve might become tired of him – "satiate", as Milton puts it, of "much converse" – though he is never weary of her. It is a small but telling imbalance in the relationship. He is tempted to allow a play – separation - a dark "retirement" – to refresh the relationship:

...to short absence I could yield
For solitude sometimes is best society,
And short retirement urges sweet return.
[IX. 428-30]

Eve, too, is under a telling misapprehension, which makes her behave "as one who loves, and some unkindness meets". She believes that Adam does not have enough faith in her; and is upset by the very idea that he thinks she might be more at risk than him:

> *Thoughts, which how found they harbour in thy breast,*
> *Adam, misthought of her to thee so dear.*
> *[IX. 288-9]*

Her syntax, tangled by indignation, inadvertently reveals the tangled truth. She thinks he is 'mis-thinking' in showing distrust of her, but she is doing at least as much 'mis-thinking' in imputing this distrust to him. She doesn't trust him to trust her – and that will be "dear" (costly) to him... If the chief accusation to be made against Eve is that she trusts in herself too much, and Adam that he trusts in himself too little, Milton is careful not to oversimplify. As with all domestic quarrels, there is a subtext in Adam and Eve's of domination and submission. These, in our fallen world, have their dark side, but in *Paradise Lost* the pleasures of this "youthful dalliance" [IV. 338] are consensual. When Eve playfully exerts her power, and Adam playfully lets her, both enjoy it, because both know that both will enjoy the moment (which both know will come) when she yields.

How artful is Eve?

The ambiguous possibilities within the innocent pleasures of dalliance are suggested in the scene where Eve physically leaves Adam. Misunderstandings have taken the argument fractionally beyond play, with hurt feelings on both sides. Eve has had her way through passive aggression: she "persisted, though submiss" – a typically perceptive psychological insight – and is described in the iconic moment when she withdraws her hand from Adam's:

Thus saying, from her husband's hand her hand
Soft she withdrew, and like a wood nymph light
Oread or dryad, or of Delia's train,
Betook her to the groves, but Delia's self
In gait surpassed and goddess-like deport,
Though not as she with bow and quiver armed,
But with such gardening tools as art yet rude
Guiltless of fire had formed, or angels brought.
[IX. 385-93]

This is a delicately balanced piece of poetry, depicting a relationship in a delicate state of balance. Eve, walking away from Adam, seems all too aware of his eyes upon her: that self-reflexive verb "betook", the marginally too-civilised "deport"... There is a hint of giddiness, of almost-floating, in her "light" gait. Being goddess-like is not yet quite how she thinks of herself, but her *amour propre* is precarious. And one of the questions raised by this complicated metaphor is of how manipulative Eve is being in her strategic withdrawal.

How artful is she? She has at her disposal only primitive tools formed by "art yet rude/ Guiltless of fire", and her techniques of flirtation are similarly unsophisticated, uncorrupted and innocent, yet the suggestion of "art" is still there. In another way, of course, we want her to be *more* artful, better armed. A bow and arrow would be a better defence against danger. She is appallingly vulnerable in her innocent self-possession.

Adam, watching her leave, is a complicit observer: he is the one who is admiring her as "goddess-like". And Milton makes plain that the pretty assertion of independence which will be so dangerous to Eve is precisely what delights Adam. That dangerously long simile as she sashays away merges into Adam's dangerously "long" gaze of adoration:

> *Her long with ardent look his eye pursued*
> *Delighted, but desiring more her stay...*
>
> *[IX. 397-8]*

Post-Fall, Eve's consciousness of her hold over Adam loses its innocence. Love play warps into power play. She becomes thoroughly aware that

Adam might be perversely excited by yielding to her. When she is wondering whether to share the fruit with him, or to "keep the odds of knowledge in my power", she imagines how becoming equal or even "sometime / Superior" could act "the more to draw his love", "a thing not undesirable". She gains the instincts of a dominatrix, yet is not entirely unsympathetic. In her post-Fall state, for the first time, the difference between the sexes makes her feel inadequate: the power gained from the fruit will "add what wants / In female sex". [IX. 820-5] She never thought herself 'wanting' before the Fall, but now she is thinking of herself, just as Adam will, as a "fair defect of nature". The harmony of a hierarchy as free from grudging or envy as it is from tyranny or pride is lost for ever.

All that prevents her from keeping the fruit for herself is a fit of proleptic jealousy. She imagines that if she dies, and Adam does not, he will be free to marry again. Her agony at the thought – "a death to think" – testifies to her love, yet this is now a love that would rather make sure her husband dies with her than let him find happiness elsewhere:

> *...confirmed then I resolve,*
> *Adam shall share with me in bliss or woe:*
> *So dear I love him, that with him all deaths*
> *I could endure, without him live no life.*
>
> *[IX. 830-3]*

Like all post-Fall states, this is a bleak, dark distortion of noble emotions. The "glorious trial of exceeding love" [X. 961] she proposes is a suicide pact.

What happens to Adam and Eve after the Fall?

Milton's poetic imagination is most intensely engaged by the great central act of choice in *Paradise Lost*; but, of course, the poem does not end with the Fall. The last three books show how Adam and Eve, unlike Satan, escape from the toils of despair and regain a modicum of choice. The delay in these last books is the stay in execution of the sentence, in which God's "permissive will" allows a space for repentance – the opportunity which Satan did not or could not take.

Immediately after the Fall, Adam and Eve fall into bitter and sterile mutual recriminations, a codependency of hatred. This rapidly passes into self-loathing: blame turns into guilt, with Adam, in particular, depicted in the grip of Satanic despair. He sounds like Satan upon Mount Niphates: the "fierce reflux" of self-accusation offers no release, and "evil conscience" (awareness of guilt) drives him only deeper into an "abyss of fears / And horrors", in which he is "from deep to deeper plunged". [X. 842-4]

Tellingly, Milton allows Eve to make the crucial breakthrough. Her passionate plea to Adam for forgiveness shows the way to escape from despair. She offers to try to take all the blame herself, and her selfless love begins the wavering path to repentance. She does so "with tears that ceased not flowing / And tresses all disordered"; but her disordered tresses, as she sobs on Adam's feet, will entangle him to good ends. A "creature so fair his reconcilement seeking" "disarms" Adam's anger, and her example moves him towards seeing the need to implore forgiveness of God.

En route, Eve offers one dead end solution: she suggests sexual abstinence, and childlessness, as a way of avoiding bringing "into this cursed world a woeful race". If abstinence is too hard – it is literally hellish "with desire to linger without hope" – suicide is the quickest way to end such "misery / And torment". Adam, however, has already moved on. He sees that her "contempt of life and pleasure", though it has its noble, Stoic side, is really a mark of "anguish and regret". Abstaining from sex is a sort of death wish.

And it is through fertility, and through Eve, that the final process of healing will be achieved; through the "seed" of a woman – Mary, the 'second Eve' – that all will at last be put right. This is why Eve is given the final word in *Paradise Lost*: she carries the hopes of humanity.

All that is to come. Adam's history lesson from

Raphael, showing him the future, is a part of a Arminian-humanist programme of rehabilitation – education, as Milton wrote, "repairs the ruins of our first parents". There is plenty that is interesting in the lessons, particularly in their application to 17th-century politics, yet for modern readers it may be here that the "want of human interest" is most seriously felt.

The ending of *Paradise Lost* however, is deeply human. It is haunted by a sense of absolute loss – that awareness of "immortality blighted" – that is truly tragic; yet it is also, precariously, a new beginning. Adam and Eve rejoin hands, a mending of their marriage, and step out as a couple – a single "solitary" unit – into the future that we share:

The world was all before them, where to choose
Their place of rest, and providence their guide:
They hand in hand, with wandering steps and slow,
Through Eden took their solitary way.
[XII. 646-9]

"The world was all before them, where to choose...": our humanity lies in choice.

Why have so many critics misread *Paradise Lost*?

This study of *Paradise Lost* has argued that Milton's greatness lies in his ability to look deeply into the human heart, and to explore the dark and mysterious 'counter-logical' impulses prompting a wrong-doing that not just apparently but actually is 'causeless'. Perhaps no other English poet – even Shakespeare – has ever stared so long and hard into the abyss "between the acting of a dreadful thing/ And the first motion", and suggested how staring too long and too hard can itself become a negative 'causeless cause', precipitating the primal *acte gratuit*.

Milton is the greatest poet ever to explore the psychology of delay. That might sound like faint praise (which other poets have specifically written about delay?), until one thinks of the extent to which delay is not only central to our human experience, but also intrinsic to poetry. Poems are written retrospectively (so delay can be liberating as well as dangerous). Aspects of delay – longing, hope, absence, and nostalgia – prompt and shape all writing. Milton, structuring his great poem about slow-motion 'delayed moments', explores both the counter-human impulses that underlie all decision-making, and the choices-beyond-choice that inform poetry.

Arguing that Milton's great poem is rooted in

human experience runs counter to several dominant strands of criticism. Critics throughout the ages have been alienated by the sheer strangeness of *Paradise Lost*. Many have misread it, assuming it was trying to be something it is not; and not recognising that its difference was part of its greatness.

In many cases, the poem was judged as a failed drama. Samuel Johnson – a superb critic of Shakespeare – read it as a play, lacking 'action' (plot) and 'manners' (character in action). And, of course, as a drama, the poem would be woefully inadequate. Read *Paradise Lost* for the dramatic suspense and, as Johnson said of another notoriously slow work, Richardson's *Clarissa*, "your impatience would be so much fretted that you would hang yourself".

Johnson saw Milton's humanity and poetry as warped by his radical politics and personal arrogance; later critics, such as A.J. Waldock and William Empson (see p.154), thought that his genius was deformed by the stranglehold of Christian 'orthodoxy'. But Waldock and Empson too were reading the poem with a mistaken emphasis upon 'plot' and 'character'. Waldock, objecting to the lack of coherent development in the character of Satan, was reading *Paradise Lost* as a novel (a genre yet to be developed in the 17th century). Empson, one of the most perceptive and humanely sympathetic of critics, similarly concentrated on the 'character' of not only Satan but also God (remarkably like Stalin, in his opinion).

Empson's conclusion, that Milton's imagination and human sympathies are fettered by Christian orthodoxy, is, however, distinctly odd. There is nothing 'off-the-peg' about Milton's Christianity. He was a non-churchgoer, and fiercely unorthodox. He believed, indeed, that any truths held only because they are 'orthodox' count as 'heresies'. And just how many other puritan-humanist-Arminian-Arian-monists can one dredge up, even out of the theologically muddied waters of the Civil War? Milton's peculiar theology, for good or bad, is uniquely his own.

So too is Milton's 'Grand Style'. Another strand of critical thinking asserted that Milton's poetry,

WILLIAM EMPSON

William Empson's attack on Paradise Lost in Milton's God (1961) is still the best ever written, though it is an attack upon Milton's Christianity rather than his poetry or personality. As a poet and man, indeed, Empson praises Milton. He regards him sympathetically as a human of extraordinary intelligence and integrity entrapped in a system of belief of extraordinary inhumanity. Christianity, according to Empson, is "evil." He finds no way of reconciling God's omniscience and omnipotence with a God of mercy. A God who foresaw the falls of Satan and of Adam and Eve, and could have stopped them, but and therefore his human sympathies, were warped by his learning. Leavis and T.S. Eliot were the best-known proponents of this view. Once again, implicit dramatic criteria underlay their assumptions: the claim that the human heart is most directly explored through language that comes close to 'ordinary human speech.' Christopher Ricks, in perhaps the single most brilliant work of Miltonic criticism, demonstrated in *Milton's Grand Style* that the distance of *Paradise Lost* from ordinary human speech did not limit, but – with its "fluid syntax", allowing multi-layered meanings – liberated his poetry.

It is this liberating distance from drama, and difference even from conventional epic, that Milton exploits throughout *Paradise Lost.* The

chose instead to condemn Satan to eternal torment and offer up his innocent Son as a barbaric blood-sacrifice is, in Empson's view, "very wicked". God, indeed, is "astonishingly like 'Uncle Joe Stalin'".

Paradise Lost is then written because Milton is "struggling to make his God appear less wicked", and Empson finds him to be remarkably successful, in the circumstances. But it is a struggle doomed to only partial success because of Milton's integrity as a poet: his "loyalty" to his text, and the "penetration" with which he probes the most problematic areas. This, for Empson, is the "chief source of [the] fascination and poignancy" of *Paradise Lost,* which he found both "horrible and wonderful". It is Empson's ambiguous admiration that gives his criticism power: he engages with the poetry in passionate and illuminating detail.◆

poem is freed from 'action' and 'manners' to work indirectly, through slow-motion effects, and digressive similes, building up echoes, and parallels, and multiple allusions, circling around and glancing at that central act of mis-choice. Ultimately, this act can perhaps only be explored indirectly and undramatically, since it is a sort of non-choice, taken for non-reasons. Milton is delving into realms that cannot be reached through drama – the "darkness visible" of counter-logical impulses within the human heart.

CHRONOLOGY

1608 (9th December) Born in The Spreadeagle, Bread Street, London. His father, John, was a scrivener (i.e. notary, money-lender and contract lawyer), and an excellent musician.

1620 Entered St Paul's School.

1625 Went up to Christ's Church, Cambridge, where his nickname was 'The Lady of Christ's'.

[27th March: Accession of Charles I]

1632 Takes MA. Lives in Hammersmith, reading.

1634 *Comus* acted

1638 *Lycidas* published. Tours France and Italy,

meeting many famous scholars (including the exiled Arminian Hugo Grotius, and the imprisoned astronomer Galileo).

1641 Publishes first pamphlets: four antiprelatical tracts (against church rule by bishops).

1642 Marries Mary Powell. She returns home within about two months.

[September: Civil War begins]

1643 *Doctrine and Discipline of Divorce* published.

1644 *Of Education* and *Areopagitica* published. Sight begins to deteriorate.

1645-6 Publication of *Poems of Mr John Milton*, Both English and Latin (registered 1645; published Jan. 1646).

1649 [30th Jan Charles I executed]

The Tenure of Kings and Magistrates published, defending regicide on the grounds that kings held authority only within an implicit contract with the people. Rulers who violate the contract are not kings but 'tyrants'.

Offered post as Secretary for the Foreign Tongues (Latin Secretary) to the Council of State *Eikonoclastes* published (commissioned by the regime as a response to the royalist propaganda, *Eikon Basilike*).

1651 *Pro Populo Anglicano Defensio* published: commissioned by Parliament to answer charges of regicide set out by Salmasius.

1652 Milton by now blind . First wife and only son die.

1653 [April: Cromwell dissolves Rump Parliament; rules as military dictator. December: Cromwell installed as Protector]

1654 *Defensio Secundo* published, justifying the dictatorship – with reservations.

1656 Marries second wife (Katherine Woodcock). Still translating for the Council, despite blindness.

1658 Released from State duties, and probably begins work on *Paradise Lost*

[3rd Sept: Cromwell dies; succeeded by his son, Richard.]

1659 [April: Army demand separation of civil and military power; May: Richard Cromwell abdicates].

A flurry of pamphlets (*Treatise of Civil Power; The Likeliest Means to Remove Hirelings out of the Church*)

[Rump Parliament restored]

1660 [Long Parliament restored]

Milton's brave, last-ditch republican pamphlet, *The Ready and Easy Way to Establish a Free*

Commonwealth published in March. He goes into hiding in a friend's house in May.

[29th May: Charles II accedes]
Milton threatened with exclusion from general pardon, but escapes.

Milton nevertheless arrested and imprisoned. Released 15th December, but with exorbitant jail fees.

1663 Marries third wife, Elizabeth Minshull.

1667 First edition of *Paradise Lost* published, in ten books.

1671 *Paradise Regained* and *Samson Agonistes* published.

1674 Second edition of *Paradise Lost* published: revised version in twelve books.

Dies in Bunhill House.

Third wife dies.

[3rd Sept: Cromwell dies; succeeded by his son, Richard.]

FURTHER READING

"Of making many books there is no end; and much study is a weariness of the flesh"
[Ecclesiastes, 12.12]

A proper bibliography of Milton's critics would add many pages to this short book.

There is one book, however, which cannot be recommended too highly, and which almost pre-empts the need to recommend any particular critics. Alistair Fowler's magnificent edition of *Paradise Lost* (Longman Annotated English Poets; revised second edition 2007) is a superb work of scholarship. It is the very Bible of Milton scholarship, containing all things necessary for most students. The notes to the poetry provide synopses of the main lines of critical debate, with references that allow the reader to trace and follow up any interpretation of interest.

Read Fowler's edition, and return to it again and again. It is the nearest approach to a comprehensive overview of Miltonic criticism one can find, and a model of humane discernment.

The list that follows is intended to be the briefest possible introduction to some of the main topics .

Life

Samuel Johnson: "Life of Milton" in *Lives of the English Poets*

Even his prejudices are illuminating; and every remark is pithy.

Barbara K. Lewalski: *The Life of John Milton* (2000)
This is the best biography by a great Miltonic scholar. It traces Milton's intellectual and political thought, and his religious development, as background to his poetry. Unsurpassed.

A.N. Wilson: *The Life of John Milton*
A lively but unscholarly account. Shorter than Lewalski!

Milton and the Romantics
Joseph Wittreich: *The Romantics on Milton*
This is such a huge and proliferating topic that I strongly recommend going back to sources. This book offers fine compendium of original Romantic reactions, ranging from essays to reported asides. A big book; but easy to trawl for illuminating quotations.

Milton's Theology
A.J. Waldock: *Paradise Lost and its Critics* (1974)
One of the first twentieth century critics to state that Milton "obviously"sympathized with Satan, so that the "official account" of his Christianity intrudes as a jarring afterthought.

William Empson: *Milton's God* (1965)
Acknowledged his debt to Waldock. Still the best attack ever written upon the theology (and humanity) of *Paradise Lost.* Empson sees Christianity as "evil"; and God, who could have prevented the Fall, as "astonishingly like 'Uncle Joe Stalin'". Milton is then, admirably but ambiguously, "struggling to make his God appear less wicked". Always superbly engaged , because of the passionate humanity – and deeply ambiguous admiration -with which he engages with Milton. Should be read by every student of *Paradise Lost.*

Dennis Danielson: *Milton's Good God: A Study in Literary Theodicy* (1982)
This gives a straightforward orthodox reply to the theological conundrums posed by Empson, and should be read, if only as

a corrective to *Milton's God*. As a critic, Empson wins on more than points. He is more lucid and passionate, far wittier and more obviously text-based than his opponent .This does not mean that he is necessarily right.

S.B. Dobranski and John P Rumrich: *Milton and Heresy* (1998)
For students who want to know how and in what way Milton might have qualified as a heretic, this is a useful guide. It suggests, indeed, that straight forward orthodox replies to theological conundrums are not Milton's stock-in-trade.

Stanley Fish: *Surprised by Sin: the Reader in Paradise Lost* (1967)
I have included this in the 'theology' section since this is a weird and controversial though extremely literary reply to Waldock and Empson. Fish argued that Milton deliberately lured us into sympathizing with Satan, so that as readers we may be "surprised into sin" and thereby become aware of our own fallen natures. As *De Doctrina Christiana* makes clear, Milton, however, does not believe that God ever deliberately 'tempts' us to fall, even for our own good. Would Milton ever want to go beyond God?

Milton's Style
F.R. Leavis: "Milton's Verse" (*Scrutiny* 1933)
The most swingeing assault upon Milton's style ever written, inditing "the extreme and callous remoteness of Milton's medium from any English that ever was spoken". "Mere orotundity", and "the routine gesture" fall into "the foreseen thud", "the routine thump."

T.S.Eliot: 'Milton I'; contributed to *Essays and Studies of the English Association* (1936) as' 'A note on the verse of Milton'

Milton's theology was repellent; his personality "unsatisfactory"; but he was most to be condemned as a "bad influence" on poetry. "The syntax is determined...by the auditory imagination, rather than by the attempt to follow actual patterns or speech or thought."

Christopher Ricks: *Milton's Grand Style* (1963)
One of the freshest and most inspiring works of criticism ever written upon *Paradise Lost.* This book allowed a whole new generation of readers to see Milton afresh as a poet who created infinitely "subtle and delicate" effects in his verse, largely through his "fluid syntax" , and the surprising linguistic resurrections embedded in his previously reviled 'Latinsims'.

INDEX

First published in 2012 by
Connell Guides
Spye Arch House
Spye Park
Lacock
Chippenham
Wiltshire SN15 2PR

10 9 8 7 6 5 4 3 2 1

Picture credits:
p.5 © Bridgeman
p.15 © Bridgeman
p.23 © Bridgeman
p.29 © Corbis
p.39 © Bridgeman
p.40 © Bridgeman
p.59 © Getty
p.65 © Bridgeman
p.77 © Alamy
p.79 © Bridgeman
p.83 © Lebrecht

A CIP catalogue record for this book is available from the British Library.
ISBN 978-1-907776-10-6

Design © Nathan Burton
Assistant Editor: Katie Sanderson
Printed in Great Britain by Butler Tanner and Dennis

www.connellguides.com